Find a Spa...

A Primary Teacher's Guide to Physical Education and Health-Related Exercise

Stephen Pain, Lawry Price,
Graham Forest-Jones and Jo Longhurst

with illustrations by
Keith Yarker

Publishe ... ondon

David Fulton Publishers Ltd
2 Barbon Close, London WC1N 3JX

First published in Great Britain by
David Fulton Publishers Ltd 1997

British Library Cataloguing in Publication Data

A catalogue record for this book is available from the British Library

ISBN 1–85346–452–X

This book has been produced using materials originally developed using funding provided in 1993 by the Health Education Authority, Hamilton House, Mabledon Place, London WC1H 9TX.

Typeset by The Harrington Consultancy, London
Printed in Great Britain by Bell and Bain Ltd, Glasgow

Contents

Introduction – Guide to using *Find a Space!*

These materials are for teachers. We called them *Find a Space!* because we think it is so important that schools find enough space in the curriculum to teach physical education properly. 'Find a space' is often what we ask children to do when they go into the hall or playground for a lesson.

Many teachers will have seen or used the *Happy Heart* materials developed by Mike Sleap and his colleagues at the University of Hull. Their materials contain good practical activity ideas which you can use in many ways. The underlying concepts in *Find a Space!* draw heavily on the work done by Len Almond and the project team of the HEA/PEA Health and Physical Education Project at Loughborough University. We have also considered carefully the work of the HEA's Primary School Project at Southampton University where Trefor Williams, Noreen Wetton and Alysoun Moon produced the excellent planning guide and classroom materials *Health for Life*. All of these resources have a common thread which is to do with looking after ourselves and learning about influences on health. So *Find a Space!* needs to be thought of as part of a planned health education programme as well as part of the PE curriculum.

The materials are intended to help teachers in primary schools teach about health-related exercise, within a well-planned physical education programme. There are references to other curriculum areas where links and overlaps can be useful, and there are suggestions for preparation and follow-up work on physical education in the classroom. But the main thrust of the work is in the practical physical activity within PE. We have not attempted to provide a complete guide to the National Curriculum in PE; but the materials are written with the National Curriculum in mind and we think they are consistent with good practice. We hope these materials will help you teach a very important part of the National Curriculum at Key Stages 1 and 2.

Using Find a Space!

The materials are in five chapters with an appendix:

Chapter 1 – *Guide to the National Curriculum: the place of health-related exercise in PE and in schools.* Teachers who have little background in physical education or sport will find this first chapter provides helpful background to the rest of the materials. All teachers should find the guide to the National Curriculum useful. It describes very simply what you need to do in plain terms free of jargon. This chapter provides the 'why' of the materials very simply and leads on to the second chapter which gives important information about health, exercise and fitness.

Chapter 2 –*Components of Health-Related Exercise.* The four main components of fitness are stamina, strength, suppleness and body composition (or energy balance). This chapter explains why each of these is important and how they are interlinked. It clarifies what kinds of exercise are most suitable for developing each of these qualities. It explains the links between health and fitness and why health-related exercise is important even for very young children. We also explain some important points about safety and this is a section which all teachers should read. There are general safety points and then specific guidance about some common exercises which should be avoided, with safer alternatives.

This chapter also maps out how the different areas of activity in National Curriculum PE (athletics, dance, games, gymnastics, outdoor and adventurous activities and swimming) can contribute to health-related exercise and explains why it is unrealistic to focus on aspects of fitness in isolation.

Chapter 3 – *Warming up and Cooling Down.* These aspects of exercise are given a separate chapter because they are very important and often neglected. We also thought it would be convenient for teachers to have the explanations for warming up and cooling down together with a bank of ideas to dip into for particular lessons. With this chapter you can read the explanations first and then come back for lesson ideas whenever you need them.

Chapter 4 – *Where to Start.* This chapter sets out some simple ideas for finding out where you are in your own school before you begin a new focus on health-related exercise. What does the school do well? Are there elements of the National Curriculum not yet covered? Is everyone as confident as they might be in teaching about health and exercise? Do all pupils have opportunities for exercise and sport outside lessons as well as in lesson time? Are there links outside the school to extend the range of opportunities for children and adults? Ways of tackling these and other questions are suggested.

Chapter 5 –*Practical Lesson Suggestions for the Six Areas of Activity in the National Curriculum.* This chapter is the core of the materials. We have written lessons for infant pupils (Key Stage 1) and junior pupils (Key Stage 2) in the contexts of athletics, dance, games, gymnastics, outdoor and adventurous activities and swimming. This should give you a basis for planning what you want the children to learn and assessing their progress. We have also picked out the aspects of the programmes of study which relate to health-related exercise. This is to help you keep these in mind during the lesson. For each example lesson you are taken stage by stage through preparing your equipment and materials; your classroom preparation with the children; getting organised in the working space; warming up; the main content or theme; points to watch during the lesson; cooling down at the end, and follow-up work afterwards. We suggest some questions to help you judge how successful the lesson was, and what to do next. Some links with other work in the classroom are suggested and we provide ideas for extension work for more able pupils as well as progression ideas for the whole class. There are also suggestions about assessing children's progress. This will help you with further planning and reporting effectively to parents.

We have provided sample lessons to enable you to see how health-related exercise can be emphasised within the PE curriculum. We have not provided a complete scheme of work or syllabus for the whole PE programme. Remember that this aspect of PE makes an important contribution to health education in the wider sense and needs to be considered in connection with other aspects such as nutrition and keeping safe. These lessons represent examples of the type of planning which we think will be most useful. We suggest you think of each example as one lesson within a unit of six. We have also provided complete outlines of units of work for two areas of activity – games and gymnastics – showing how the work might progress.

1 Guide to the National Curriculum: the place of health-related exercise in PE and in schools

The National Curriculum as revised in 1995 is in three main parts: General Requirements, Programmes of Study and End of Key Stage Descriptions.

General Requirements for Physical Education Key Stages 1–4.

There are no attainment targets as such in PE. The General Requirements emphasise the practical nature of PE and begin by setting out the intention that PE 'should involve all pupils in a continuous process of planning, participating in and performing physical activity'. The original proposal of the National Curriculum Working Group for PE was to have three explicit attainment targets: planning, performing and evaluating physical activity. Planning and evaluating have been absorbed into what is in effect a single attainment target to emphasise the practical nature of the subject. However it is important that planning and evaluating (and understanding about exercise generally) are given full emphasis. The General Requirements across all key stages set out three important areas of learning in addition to the practical performance. These are:

1. to promote physically active and and healthy lifetyles;
2. to develop positive attitudes;
3. to ensure safe practice.

We suggest that these things have to be actually taught and discussed. We don't think children will *necessarily* learn them from taking part in, say, games or gymnastics. That is why we have set out background explanations which will, we hope, help you to teach these fundamental aspects of PE.

The National Curriculum in PE covers six areas of activity: athletic activities, dance, games, gymnastic activities, outdoor and adventurous activities and swimming.

This is how the National Curriculum Order describes what is to be covered in the primary school:

- *Key Stage 1 – In each year of the key stage,* pupils should be taught three areas of activity: games, gymnastic activities and dance, using indoor and outdoor environments where appropriate. In addition schools may choose to teach swimming in Key Stage 1 using the programme of study set out in Key Stage 2.
- *Key Stage 2* – Pupils should be taught six areas of activity. *During each year of the key stage* pupils should be taught games, gymnastic activities and dance. At points during the key stage pupils should be taught athletic activities, outdoor and adventurous activities, and unless they have already completed the programme of study for swimming during Key Stage 1, swimming. If aspects of the swimming programme of study have been taught during Key Stage 1, pupils should be taught the Key Stage 2 programme of study starting at the appropriate point.

Programmes of Study and End of Key Stage Descriptions

These set out the aspects of health and exercise which should be taught throughout the key stage. For Key Stage 1 children should be taught:

- about the changes that occur to their bodies as they exercise;
- to recognise the short-term effects of exercise on the body.

There is a very brief outline of the areas of activity for each key stage (three at Key Stage 1 and six at Key Stage 2). For example the programme of study in gymnastics for Key Stage 1 consists of the following:

a. different ways of performing the basic actions of travelling using hands and feet, turning, rolling, jumping, balancing, swinging and climbing, both on the floor and using apparatus;
b. to link a series of actions both on the floor and and using apparatus, and how to repeat them.

Through the teaching of the programmes of study children are expected to meet learning objectives which are set out in End of Key Stage Descriptions. There are no level descriptions at eight levels (with an additional level for exceptional performance) as there are currently in the core subjects, technology, history and geography. End of Key Stage Descriptions are very general expectations of what pupils should be able to do by the end of each Key Stage – for example 'plans and performs simple skills safely, and shows control in linking actions together'. Schools will need to think through what this kind of general description might mean for an individual child. For example: 'I can run, jump, roll and show a balance' in gymnastics. Clearly there is scope for these descriptions to be interpreted in different ways – both to meet the varying needs of children of different abilities and to allow to some extent for the differing strengths of teachers.

There is also a need to find ways of describing *quality* in what children achieve (in other words, how well do they do things). This is important so that we can ensure that children are achieving as much as they can and so that we can report usefully to parents. It is also important to assess how children are doing in relation to what we expect the majority of children to achieve. OFSTED inspectors make judgements about standards of achievements in relation to 'national expectations'. It is important that teachers have a reasonable idea about how well children are doing without making unhelpful comparisons between children or creating situations in which children feel they are failing.

Teachers will have to decide for themselves the detail of what they want children to learn. This will mean mapping out proper schemes of work in much more detail than in the programmes of study. It will involve working out what activities to provide (and how much time and emphasis to give to each) so that children can acquire and develop appropriate skills, knowledge and confidence. It will also mean developing effective ways of assessing how well the children are doing. The original non-statutory guidance from 1992 is helpful in this respect and there are examples of planning a unit of work (for, say, 6 weeks) and how units of work build up into schemes of work for a whole key stage. The examples given illustrate very well how progression can be developed.

The Programmes of Study build on much of what many schools are doing already. For these schools it will be a matter of identifying gaps rather than starting from the very beginning. The Programmes of Study and End of Key Stage Descriptions are very broad and general. For schools where teachers are confident in PE there will be little difficulty in implementing them. In schools where PE is less well developed it may be that the lack of detail in the Programmes of Study will mean that they provide little help in planning a programme. There is a lot of practical help with planning in the original non-statutory guidance. Also teachers will find it very useful to refer to the interim and final reports of the National Curriculum PE working party. These reports provide detailed information and background material not included in the final National Curriculun Order. In particular the interim report provided examples of ten levels of attainment which children might achieve in each area of activity. This may be helpful in planning and assessment.

Some primary schools have access to a learner pool and will therefore be able to begin to teach swimming at the infant stage. Most schools will teach swimming in Key Stage 2 because they are likely to be using local authority facilities which are more suitable for older children. Many schools are deciding to limit the amount of swimming taught because of financial constraints. Swimming as a medium for teaching about health and fitness is probably more appropriate for Key Stage 2. Hopefully schools, despite pressures of time and money, will not take the specific target of being able to swim 25 metres as the end point of their swimming programmes. Children should clearly be able to swim more strongly than that and swimming is, after all, an important learning experience. We don't stop the teaching of reading after a minimum level has been reached and it is no more sensible to do so with swimming. Swimming is an essential survival skill, as well as a wonderful way of helping children build healthy bodies, and an enjoyable way of keeping fit throughout life. Swimming should be in the curriculum and schools should find ways to keep it there.

We demonstrate how the principles of health-related exercise can be emphasised in all the areas of activity. All physical activity results in energy expenditure and hopefully some enjoyment. But the important feature of health-related exercise is that it is *planned* to have beneficial effects on stamina, suppleness, strength and body composition and therefore on a person's health. Children experience a variety of sports and games in school and there are underlying messages about health-related exercise which children should be helped to understand. This can be done partly as a result of taking part in the six areas of activity in the 'permeation model' proposed by the SCAA (School Curriculum and Assessment Authority) in the PE Order. Ensuring effective teaching about health-related exercise needs specific planning and effective use of time and facilities. We believe that the process of planning can lead to a better understanding of the value of PE in the primary school. This can play a part in helping children to develop a positive attitude to physical education and exercise.

The Place of Health-Related Exercise in PE

PE should enable children to develop physical skills. It should build on children's natural delight in movement. It should provide opportunities for challenge, creativity, co-operation and competition. PE can also be the context for many aspects of social development – for example, working in groups and teams, exploring the nature of individual capabilities, learning about the development of sports and games and their rules and etiquette. PE should provide planned regular exercise of different kinds to assist healthy growth and physical development. Children should find satisfaction and enjoyment from taking part in exercise and this experience of exercise should be linked to the development of appropriate knowledge about our bodies and why we need to look after them. We achieve these aims, or many of them, by providing a variety of experiences of games, dance, gymnastics, swimming and so on. The activities themselves are important, and children should have a broad and effective education about the various forms of physical activity. They are also the contexts in which 'education about the physical' takes place. Children's physical development is important for its own sake. But children's knowledge and understanding also need to be developed so that they can be well-informed participants in physical activity. Their skill development is vital in giving them access to participation in physical activity while at school and for the rest of their lives.

Excellence of performance and competitive success for children at school have a valuable place and the value is increased enormously if participation is extended into adult life. This is more likely if competitive sport in schools is planned to include as many children as possible and is presented in appropriate forms. We need to keep in mind the differences in children's physical abilities and different rates of maturation which can have a geat effect on how much children enjoy taking part. Children's basic fitness varies enormously. Some children are able to carry out sustained vigorous exercise without discomfort. Other children will find relatively low levels of activity can make them feel breathlesss and uncomfortable. So we need to be careful about how we present competitive activities. For example, we need to beware of expecting all children to enjoy taking part in full-scale versions of adult games. We also need to consider the effects of limiting a school's PE or extra-curricular programme to particular sports such as football. Experience of a variety of activities is essential.

PE has very important links with health education which is concerned with all aspects of health and personal development. PE as a part of health education focuses on the development and care of our physical selves. Though not everyone will be successful at sport, everyone can be good at exercise. Regular exercise (including appropriate versions of sports and games) is such an important part of healthy living that we must plan a relevant physical education curriculum – stretching the most talented, supporting the less confident and ensuring that everyone feels successful. Physical education, even for very young children, should be planned and progressive and have an appropriate emphasis on health. Every pupil's learning should be supported and monitored as carefully as their progress in reading: it is that important!

There are many aspects of school life which can affect children's attitudes to themselves. Children's feelings of physical confidence and competence may be affected strongly by their experiences in PE lessons and by other aspects of school. Chapter 4 discusses some of these issues and gives some help with these questions.

2 Components of Health-Related Exercise

Reasons why

Exercise is important for everyone's health for a number of reasons. They can be summed up by saying that if we are physically active all our body systems work more effectively and efficiently. When we exercise regularly we feel better and have more energy for everyday tasks. We are likely to be healthier and less susceptible to illnesses such as coronary heart disease, and some kinds of diabetes. But if we simply say that to children it may not seem very relevant to them. Children are much more interested in the present than in worries about their future health. And health is about more than physical fitness and freedom from disease. A broad view of health is also very much linked to people's self-image and self-esteem. Children who may not enjoy exercise very much may feel that talk about feeling good through exercise doesn't match their experience. We need to ensure that children's experience is satisfying and to avoid situations where people associate exercise with aching limbs and burning lungs on cross country runs or shivering during outdoor games lessons on cold wet days.

Left to themselves young children mostly enjoy spontaneous exercise and run about and jump and play happily for hours on end. Problems only tend to arise later when other influences intervene. The role models of adults around children are very important, and the attractions of less active pastimes such as television and computers can be very powerful. As time goes on it becomes apparent to children that some people are more able at sports and games than others. Children who are regularly overlooked or left until last when teams are being picked, may begin to feel exercise is not for them. Some children may find that PE at school puts them in situations where their low level of fitness leaves them feeling distressed and not inclined to repeat the experience.

Children become aware that people come in all sorts of shapes and sizes. We need to ensure that children realise that it is fine to be the basic shape you are, and that people of all physical types can enjoy and benefit exercise. We need to do what we can to ensure that children's views of themselves as active individuals are not undermined by messages they receive from each other, from the media or from school. Children's experience of PE and sport at school has not always been ideal. Lessons are not always planned effectively enough to give every pupil enjoyable, challenging and satisfying experiences. We should be giving appropriate teaching to all pupils. We need to reward effort and participation and we need to keep the emphasis on competition in proportion. Most teachers are aware of these issues and never intentionally give negative messages to children, but in primary schools we need to:

- Do our best to make sure that all children have positive experiences of physical activity and exercise in school.
- Begin the process of ensuring that all children understand what exercise can do for them and are able to plan an appropriate exercise programme for themselves irrespective of their sporting ability or success.

The next section gives a short explanation of the main aspects of health-related exercise in very simple language. If you want more detail as background knowledge for yourself there are useful references on page 103.

Health-related exercise can be thought of in terms of activities related to improving:

- Stamina (being able to 'keep going' at activities like running or walking briskly without getting out of breath too quickly).
- Strength (being able to exert force, i.e. lifting, pulling and pushing).
- Suppleness (having a full range of movement of joints, i.e. being able to bend and stretch easily).
- Body composition (or energy balance).
- Posture.

All of these are important but they are also connected to each other. All forms of exercise – done sensibly, safely and regularly – are good for you because they must improve at least one of these aspects of fitness. New exercise fashions emerge and fade away from time to time. Aerobics, skate boarding and roller blading are three obvious examples. Quite often such fashion booms are related to marketing of equipment, clothing or videotapes. Sometimes fashions last and sometimes they fade away quickly. So it is important to look beneath the glossy exterior and examine what a particular system actually does. There are a few simple guidelines to remember if you are thinking about a particular form of exercise (perhaps a sport or game) and you want to know if it will do you good, or if it would be suitable for children:

- Any form of regular whole-body exercise will maintain or improve your stamina (the sort of exercise that makes you slightly out of breath, sweat and makes your heart beat faster, such as brisk walking or swimming). It has been generally accepted that, for most benefit, such exercise needs to be done at least three times a week for at least 20 minutes at a time with your heart beating at 60–80% of its maximum rate. Medical experts now think that lower intensity physical activity, such as you might have on a long walk, can be just as valuable for maintaining health.
- Any form of exercise involving fairly strenuous effort against a resistance (pushing, pulling, lifting, hanging, swinging, jumping, climbing stairs) will maintain your strength, or increase it if you increase the resistance progressively.
- Any form of exercise involving slow, gentle stretching will maintain your suppleness, or increase it if you gradually increase the range of movement when you stretch.
- All ways of raising your level of activity, especially whole body exercise like running or swimming, will help you to maintain a desirable body weight, in conjunction with a sensible, balanced diet.
- Many forms of strength developing exercise and many forms of exercise focusing on harmony of the body and mind such as dance, yoga and tai' chi can help improve posture.

Stamina, strength and flexibility

Any form of exercise which uses the large muscles of your arms and legs for more than a few minutes at a time will improve your stamina or general endurance. This would include jogging or running, brisk walking, swimming, cycling, aerobics or exercise to music, many kinds of dancing, and many sports and games that involve prolonged or repeated spells of running. This is because the exercise will make your heart and circulation work harder to provide oxygen for the muscles doing the work. If you do it regularly your heart, circulation and muscles adapt to the increased demand and become more effective and efficient – you become able to do the same amount of exercise for less effort or more exercise for the same effort. For this reason it is important that children have regular, controlled experience of activities like running and swimming. They need to find these sustained forms of exercise enjoyable and satisfying because they are the basis of so many sports and games and activities. Having stamina means being able to respond to sudden extra demands of physical activity, and to keep going for long periods not just at sport but in everyday activities too. In the long term this is probably even more important than sports and games. We need to be able to walk up hills, run for a bus and carry shopping, and we need to be ready to enjoy opportunities to make the most of special occasions too, so stamina for social dancing and other forms of leisure is important.

Children think mostly in the present and don't worry too much about the future but long-term health is possibly the most serious reason why the kinds of exercise associated with improved stamina are valuable. There is now overwhelming evidence that people who are physically active, especially in stamina building exercise, have a lower risk of a heart attack or stroke, are more likely to maintain a desirable body weight, have better mental health and a positive outlook. People who exercise regularly through activities like running and swimming have a more efficient heart and circulation. For every beat of the heart their blood supplies more oxygen to the muscles including the heart itself. Fit people also have muscles which are more efficient at using oxygen. Without going into too much detail we know that regular exercise has a protective effect against coronary heart disease.

All of this illustrates why it is so important that children's experience of exercise is satisfying enough for them to want to continue it into adult life. Physical activity is a natural part of daily life which is, or should be, as habitual as sleeping and eating.

Any form of exercise which involves repeated use of particular muscles, especially against gravity, will increase the strength of those muscles. For example, regular activities like climbing a rope will make your arms and legs stronger. The nearer the effort you repeatedly make is to your maximum effort, the more you will increase strength. (This is why weight training using increasing resistance is the most efficient way for adults to increase strength systematically.) But if you do repeated exercise in this way you will also increase the ability of your muscles to keep on doing the activity. In other words you also increase the *local endurance* of those muscles. Your muscles become stronger because more muscle fibres are brought into action as the muscles become better adapted. *Local muscular endurance* improves mainly because the muscles themselves become more efficient at using the oxygen supplied to them by the blood pumped around the body by the heart. This illustrates how the components of fitness are linked.

Although specific training produces specific changes, almost any form of exercise has a number of connected effects. If you are using large muscles like those in your legs for jumping, you will also increase your *stamina* because the muscles will need a lot of oxygen and the heart will have to beat faster and more strongly to supply it. If you do the exercise regularly the heart and circulation become more efficient at the same time as you are improving the strength and local endurance of your muscles. If you run or swim regularly you will be developing the strength and local muscular endurance of your arms and legs as well as improving your general endurance or stamina. Perhaps more importantly, you will also be helping to maintain your health and be having fun too!

Stretching done safely maintains or improves *suppleness or flexibility.* Most people know some form of stretching exercise – toe touching or some other common form of limbering up. We now know that many traditional exercises are unsafe and people have begun to realise that quite a lot of the exercises taught over the years for stretching or limbering up should be done with great caution. Some are ineffective or even harmful. There are a few golden rules to remember:

1. All stretching to improve flexibility should be slow and gentle and should be done after some gentle whole body exercise like slow jogging to get the body warm and blood circulating throught the muscles. (See Chapter 3 for a more detailed explanation of warming up.)
2. The idea when stretching is to move gently towards the point where you can't reach any further and hold that position. This allows the muscles being stretched to relax and get used to gradually becoming longer.
3. No stretching exercise should be done in a way which puts strain on any of the body's joints – especially the lower back and knees. (Chapter 3 gives examples of exercises to be avoided and safer alternatives.)

So why do we need to be supple or flexible in the first place? The answer is that supple people are likely to be able to move more freely and easily and they are less likely to suffer injuries. If your leg muscles are accustomed to exercise and you have a good range of movement in the hip joints you will be able to run more freely (and probably faster) than if you are stiff or more limited in your range of movement. This would be important if you were involved in a sport where running fast is an asset. But being able to run freely also means you are more likely to enjoy it. If you have supple shoulders you are likely to be able to swim more easily (especially using front crawl or backstroke) than someone with stiff shoulders. Supple people are likely to find playing games like badminton or tennis comes more easily than for people unused to exercising. Suppleness is also vital for strenuous sports like athletics, gymnastics or judo, but for most people suppleness is more important for everyday activities like climbing a ladder, cleaning windows or reaching a high shelf. As people grow older even simple activities like pulling off a sweater or fixing one's hair can become more difficult so it is important for people to maintain the normal suppleness (and strength) of their shoulders. Suppleness needs to be maintained alongside strength and stamina.

The important thing for young children is to maintain and encourage the natural suppleness which most of them have. If you watch your class you will realise that many of them are quite supple. But even apparently normal activities like sitting on the floor with their legs crossed and backs straight will be quite difficult for some children for any length of time. Some of the children in your class will find simple gymnastic activities difficult (like kicking up to a handstand) because they have stiff lower backs and shortened hamstring muscles (the large muscles at the back of the thighs). So we need to ensure that all the children prepare properly for exercise at the beginning of every lesson by gentle warming up, and we need to encourage regular and systematic stretching to help children keep supple.

Energy balance and body composition

Everyone knows that it is a good idea to maintain a sensible body weight and not to carry too much extra fat. We all need some fat to maintain body warmth, to protect vital organs and for fuel reserves. Body composition is often expressed as a percentage of body mass as fat. Between 10 and 20% is the acceptable range for adult males and 20–30% percent for women. People who are overfat are much more likely to suffer shortness of breath and disorders such as heart disease and diabetes. Extra weight puts strain on the knees, hips and back. It is important to understand the difference between 'overweight' and 'overfat'. Doctors often use height and weight charts as a guide to desirable bodyweight and these are often published in magazines. They can be a helpful guide and take into account people's basic build (governed by the size of their bones) which varies a lot. Two people of the same height could have a considerable difference in weight and still be within their desirable limits. Some very muscular people can be considerably heavier than the weights shown in the charts because muscle is heavier than fat. Body composition is more important than weight. Obviously when working with children we have to be very sensitive and careful about dealing with body composition and related issues. Our perception of our size and shape are an important part of our self-image.

When people feel they are overweight they commonly try to lose weight by eating less – they go on a diet. This may seem to be successful, perhaps for a few weeks, as we lose a few pounds, but it is rarely successful in the long term and may actually be harmful. One factor often neglected in these unsuccessful attempts to stick to a desirable bodyweight is the influence of exercise.
Maintaining a desirable weight and shape is largely a matter of achieving the right balance between the energy coming in (food and drink) and the energy going out (mostly physical activity). Many people who are lean and active actually eat a lot – sometimes more than people who struggle with their weight. Often this doesn't seem fair and there are inherited differences in the rate at which different people use energy. However, one big difference may be the relatively large amounts of exercise which lean people have got used to. You may have seen articles saying that you have to run a marathon to lose a pound of fat. This kind of statement (which often seems to be designed to put people off exercising) is not helpful because trying to lose weight quickly is not a good idea. It is much more helpful to bear in mind that a gradual increase in your physical activity (say increasing the amount of walking you do by a small amount – perhaps half a mile a day at first) together with a balanced diet will help you to maintain an appropriate bodyweight and improve your body composition.
When you exercise, your metabolic rate (the rate at which your body is using energy) increases and it stays higher than normal for some time after the exercise. This means you are still using extra energy even when you are not exercising!

When you lose weight gradually through exercising over a longer period than a few weeks you can be reasonably sure it is mainly fat you are losing. When you lose weight through dieting alone you are probably losing liquid (water) first and then body fat and you may be losing some lean tissue as well. You can't lose more fat by sweating more – you simply put back any weight lost as soon as you have a drink.
So children need to understand how physical activity helps maintain a desirable energy balance. Increasing physical activity will not bring about dramatic weight loss, but it will help to maintain a desirable bodyweight. We said earlier how important it is to be sensitive and careful when talking about body composition and energy balance with children. We should not be aiming at weight loss as such with children. If children are overfat it is probably better (and safer) to aim to slow down weight gain (by encouraging a gentle increase in physical activity and slightly restricting energy intake) while height continues to increase so that weight for height reaches the normal range over several years.

It is equally important that children understand the importance of eating a healthy diet to maintain energy balance (i.e. low in fat and high in fibre especially fruit and vegetables). It is probably even more important to reinforce the message that people naturally come in all shapes and sizes and that is fine, as long as our body weight is within the desirable range for our height, and as long as we feel fit enough to enjoy sensible exercise. There is a great deal of influence on us all particularly from the glossy magazines and broadcast media to accept fashionable slim shapes as desirable. Obviously it is a good idea to keep our bodies in good condition but good health is the main consideration – you don't have to have a supermodel figure to be healthy. One of the most important messages we can give to our children is: that it's OK to exercise in any way you enjoy, whatever your shape, size or talent.

There is a great opportunity in the primary school to reinforce concepts of acceptance of variety and individual differences and of being comfortable with our bodies. It may be helpful to encourage children, as they become old enough to consider these things, to begin to think about what kinds of exercise might be more appropriate for different people. For example if you have a big frame or a naturally stocky build it may be a better idea to choose swimming or cycling as your regular exercise rather than running. This kind of discussion needs to be handled very sensitively because we need to be careful not to reinforce stereotypes. In the end people are likely to continue with activities they enjoy or get satisfaction from. So the main priority is to do everything we can to provide a range of positive and rewarding experiences.

Posture

Posture is another important aspect of shape. Talking about posture may bring to mind images of children in rows sitting up straight in class or doing 'drill', or 'deportment classes' for young ladies! In reality good posture isn't to do with discipline or impressing anybody: it is an important aspect of children's healthy growth and development and of our long-term health.

One reason why posture is important is that every year thousands of adults of all ages have to take time off work because of back pain. Much of this may be because of injuries caused by inefficient lifting of furniture or other heavy objects. So teaching children about safe and effective lifting techniques is very important.

It may be that we have a job that involves sitting at a desk for hours on end. If we don't take care to sit upright in a comfortable, efficient position our bodies get used to slumping over the desk with rounded shoulders or sagging back against the chair. Added to that we can develop tension in the neck and shoulders leading to headaches. From the age of 5 onwards children have a job (being at school) that involves sitting at a desk or table for increasingly long periods so we need to keep an eye on the way they sit and encourage them to sit well. It is ironic that we require them to be inactive for so much of the time when their bodies as well as their minds need activity so much.

Another aspect of everyday life that can lead to poor posture is regularly carrying a bag to and from work or school. If we always carry the load on the same shoulder we can finish up over a long period of time with uneven shoulders and possibly curvature of the spine. Given the number of other things we do in a one-sided way (writing, throwing a ball, using tools like hammers and screwdrivers, using bats and racquets) it is really important that we make sure that children develop their bodies as evenly as possible. We can help that by including some specific activities in lessons which exercise both arms and both shoulders.

A common problem connected with poor posture is weak stomach or abdominal muscles. This may be linked to being overfat, resulting in the common hollow-backed posture that can be associated with low back pain in adult life. It is essential that we include activities in our teaching to strengthen the muscles of the stomach and lower back. This may fit most naturally in the gymnastics lesson, especially in the warm-up phase. We also need to encourage all the children to sit and stand well whenever possible. This means encouraging children to think of being tall and relaxed with shoulders down and back (and not hunched up) and head held up evenly. Lack of flexibility in the hips and lower back can make it difficult or uncomfortable to sit upright (especially on the floor) so teachers need to look out for those children who find it tiring to sit up straight, or who tend to lean on one hand as often as they can.

We need to include specific stretching exercises in the warm-up phase of every lesson and sometimes in the cool-down phase to ensure that the children are getting regular opportunities to maintain and develop their flexibility. It would be very helpful for teachers to lead a few minutes of simple stretching from time to time in the classroom. This would benefit the children physically and would also help them maintain their interest in the lesson.

3 Warming Up and Cooling Down

Warming up

Reasons why

Because most young children seem to be spontaneously active and happily run about in their playtimes at school, it would be easy to think that warming up for exercise is unnecessary for children. After all, few children pull muscles in the way that adults engaged in sport or exercise sometimes do. This is probably partly because children's bodies have more elasticity than those of adults and partly because much of the time children will stay within the limits of their abilities when they engage in spontaneous play. But it is still important that children learn about the importance of preparing properly for exercise and this means learning how to warm up. Warming up at the beginning of a lesson may also help to avoid the kinds of accidental injuries that children do commonly suffer – bumps, bruises and cuts from falls and collisions. Warming up doesn't just prepare the body physically, it helps people to get into the right frame of mind to concentrate properly on the task.

It isn't just to avoid injuries that we need to warm up for exercise. There are several reasons and children should begin to understand them as early as possible.

On a purely physical level the effects of warming up are to:

- prepare the joints (hips, knees, shoulders, etc.) for the work to come;
- prepare the heart and circulation for increased work;
- prepare the muscles and nerves for the movements to be performed.

This is intended in general terms to prevent sore muscles and injury, to improve performance, to contribute to the development of good flexibility and to contribute to harmonious physical development. These general effects are brought about by a period of warming up which should consist of:

- Gentle mobilising exercises like arm swings (not stretching) within the range of normal movement.
- Low-level aerobic activities (e.g. walking, gentle jogging) gradually increasing in intensity.
- Gentle stretching exercises held ideally for 8-10 seconds. (This could be just a few seconds for young children not used to holding stretch positions. Increase the time as they get used to the exercises.)

After these three phases of warm-up children are more prepared for the demands placed on their bodies in the lesson. We need to take care to make warming up as much fun as possible. Our warm-up bank (later in this chapter) is intended to help you with ideas for that.

Some other background points about warming up which may be helpful to know:

- Rhythmic (not jerky or bouncy) exercises are good for mobilising and help release tension as well as being enjoyable.
- In all three phases of warming up the activity should begin carefully and gently and gradually increase in intensity.
- Exercises should ideally flow naturally from one to the next and the increase in intensity should lead naturally from one phase to the next.
- The exercises should promote the blood circulation and should include all parts of the body – feet, legs and hips; trunk (stomach, back and chest); hands, arms, shoulders and neck.
- Exercises should suit the age and knowledge of the class – for infants you will naturally use a lighter style; for older children perhaps more explanation and probably more self-direction.
- Warm-up activities should be designed to raise the children's heart rates gradually.
- There should be little time lag between the warm-up and the next phase of the lesson – there is little point in warming up if the children then sit down for a 10 minute explanation!

Time spent on warming up can vary depending on:

- the age of the children (more as they get older)
- the activity planned (more strenuous activity requires more warm-up)
- the conditions in the working space (temperature etc.)
- the fitness and experience of the children.

More about how

This next section provides detailed information about warming up. Warming up should include exercises for the following:

The neck

- bending the head gently forward and
- tilting the head up (called flexion and extension) (Figure 3.1).
- and turning gently to either side (called rotation) (Figure 3.2).

Figure 3.1

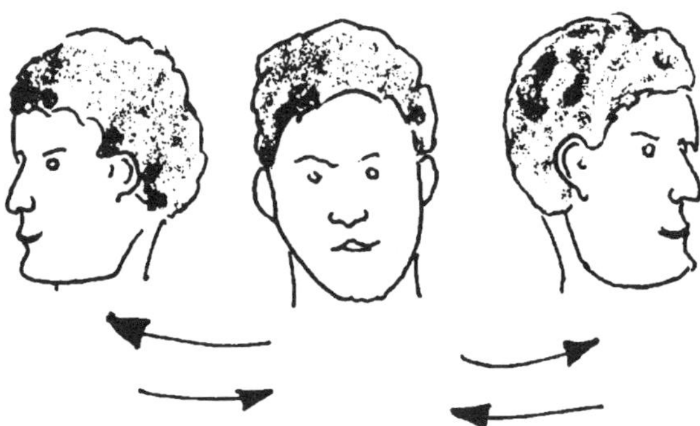

Figure 3.2

The shoulder girdle

- rolling shoulders up, down, forward and back

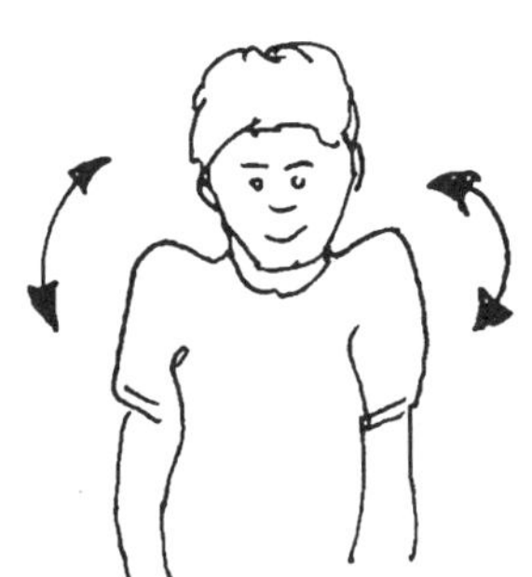

Figure 3.3

The shoulder joints

- reaching forward and up with the arms
- lifting arms up and down to the side (Figure 3.4) and across the chest (Figure 3.5),
- circling arms forwards and backwards with arms straight or hands on shoulders (Figure 3.6).

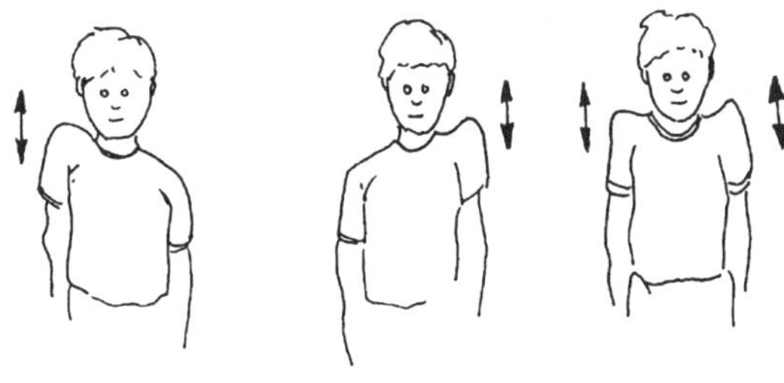

Figure 3.4

Figure 3.5

Figure 3.6

The arms:

- hands to shoulders bend and straighten arms (Figure 3.7).

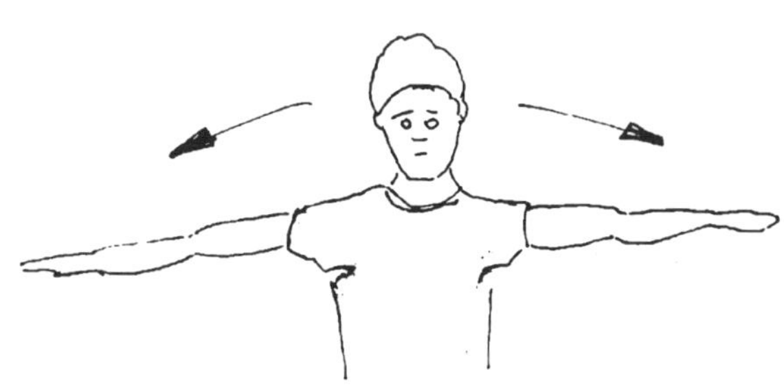

Figure 3.7

The hands and wrists

- circle wrists, bend and straighten.

The trunk

- on hands and knees – hump and hollow (Figure 3.8),
- standing up – circling hips (Figure 3.9),
- standing up – bending to the side with hands on hips and knees slightly bent,
- lying on front – hands under shoulders gently push shoulders and chest off floor.

Figure 3.8

Figure 3.9

The hips

- standing up – gently swing one leg in turn forward and back, and to the side,
- lying down on back – gently draw each knee to chest (Figure 3.10).

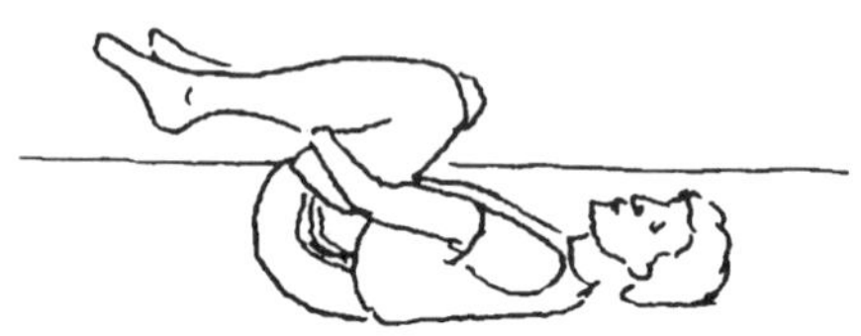

Figure 3.10

The knees

- standing up – bend and straighten knees in half squats (Figure 3.11),
- standing up – gently circle both knees in the same direction.

Figure 3.11

The ankles

- standing up – rise up and down on toes,
- sitting – circle each foot in turn,
- leaning on wall – gently stretch each calf.

Safe and Unsafe Exercises

Some exercises have been commonly performed which are now considered to be potentially harmful especially if carried out repeatedly over a long time. Some of these are well known and will have been carried out by many of us at school or in training sessions for various sports. These exercises are often described (in recent publications about sport and exercise) as 'controversial' or 'contra-indicated'. The point about them is that they place undue stress on vulnerable parts of the human body. This can lead eventually to pain, damage to joints and restriction of physical activity. Particularly vulnerable areas are the neck, lower back and knees. Potentially harmful exercises tend to involve:

- hyperextension (or extreme arching, for example of the back),
- hyperflexion (or extreme bending, for example of the knees).

Both of these can cause strain in muscles, tendons (joining muscles to bones) and ligaments (joining two bones). They can also result in undue wear and tear and long-term damage to joints.

Two other main potentially harmful activities are 'ballistic stretching' (stretching with vigorous bouncing such as bouncing toe touching) and 'high impact' exercises such as repeated jumping or hopping especially on hard surfaces.

It is important to understand what particular exercises actually do because then it is less likely that unsafe activities will be unwittingly performed. For example, many people will have carried out sit-ups with straight legs, or with their feet held under a bar or by a partner, in the belief that these are good exercises for the abdominal (stomach) muscles. In fact although there is some action by the abdominal muscles these are mainly exercises for the hip flexor muscles which join the lower spine and pelvis to the thigh bones. These exercises also create great strain on the lower back and are not to be recommended. The same applies to lying on the floor on your back and lifting up straight legs. Safer alternatives which really do exercise the abdominal muscles are shown below.

Children are particularly at risk from unsafe exercises because their bodies are immature and their bones and joints are easily damaged. Damage to the soft growth areas at the ends of children's bones can easily occur and affect their development. Most at risk are talented performers (especially in soccer, gymnastics and swimming) who may be involved in frequent training sessions, matches, and events. It is important to remember that children are not miniature adults and they need to be protected at times from excessive demands. When planning activities for children teachers need to be careful to:

1. increase the amount of exercise gradually;
2. ensure the children have adequate muscular strength and flexibility;
3. ensure all exercise is carried out in a mechanically sound way;
4. encourage the use of proper footwear and appropriate surfaces to work on.

These are the most common potentially harmful exercises. Alongside each one we have provided a safer alternative.

1. Standing toe touching

This places severe strain on the lower back – especially if you bounce up and down!

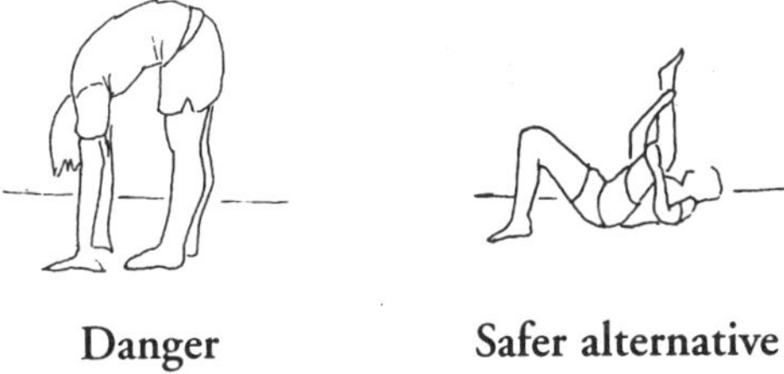

Danger (Figure 3.12 (a)) | **Safer alternative** (Figure 3.12 (b))

Lie on back, gently pull calf towards the body until you feel a mild stretch.

2. Full head circling

This can damage the small vertebrae in the neck and pinch the nerve endings.

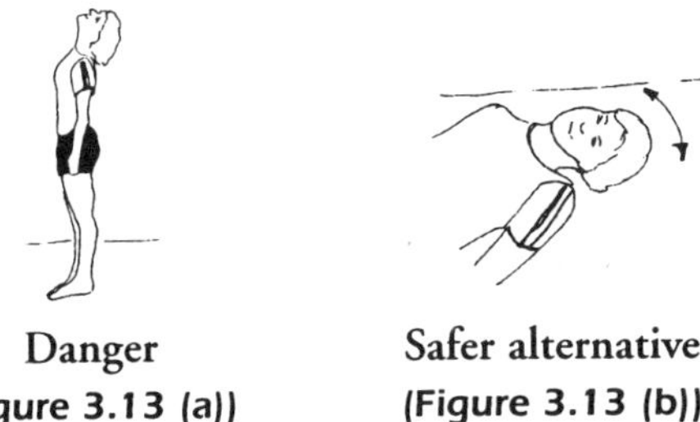

Danger (Figure 3.13 (a)) | **Safer alternative** (Figure 3.13 (b))

Lying on the floor or standing: (i) look slowly from left to right; (ii) tilt ear to shoulder; (iii) head slowly forward, chin to chest

3. Straight leg sit-ups

This places severe strain on the lower back, also if done with hands behind head can put strain on neck.

Danger (Figure 3.14 (a))

Safer alternative (Figure 3.14 (b))

Bent leg curl-ups. Do not have your feet held by a partner or under apparatus, have arms across chest or hands gently over ears – not pulling on head

4. Straight leg lifts

This places severe strain on the lower back; tends to lengthen stomach muscles and cause hollow back. It may damage discs and put pressure on nerves.

Danger (Figure 3.15 (a))

Safer alternative (Figure 3.15 (b))

Curl and extend: bring knees up to a curl shape then extend legs vertically, return legs to knees-bent position before lowering to ground

5. Hurdle stretch position

This puts strain on the ligaments of the knee of the bent leg.

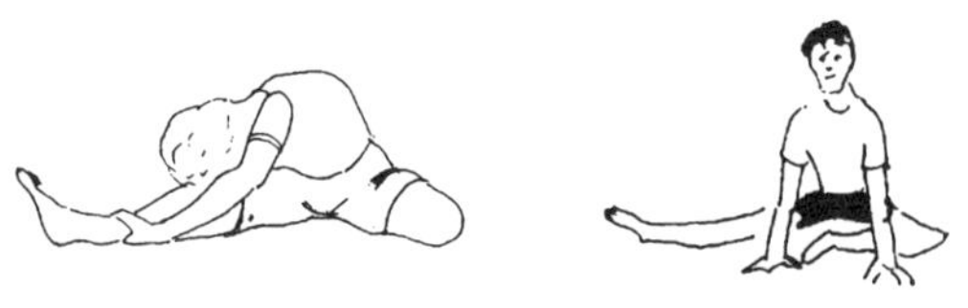

Danger (Figure 3.16 (a))

Safer alternative (Figure 3.16 (b))

Seated stretch, bent knee as shown, lean gently forward

6. Back arching

This puts strain on the spine.

(a) The cobra

Danger (Figure 3.17 (a))

Safer alternative (Figure 3.17 (b))

Cobra on elbows (support upper body on elbows and gently lift)

(b) Banana bends

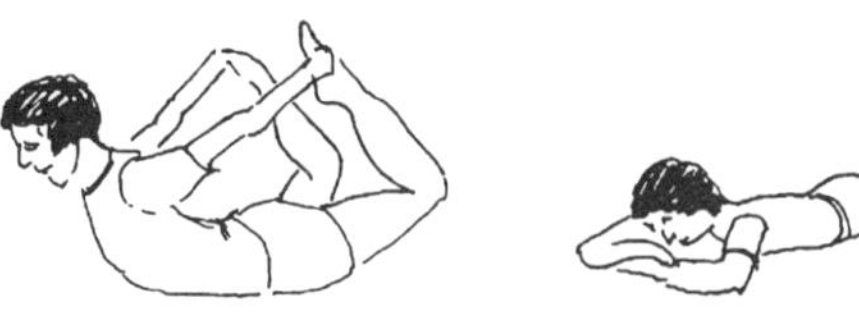

Danger (Figure 3.18 (a))

Safer alternative (Figure 3.18 (b))

Single leg lifts (keep chin resting on arms)

(Figure 3.18 (c))
Cat curl (do not let the stomach sag)

Another safer alternative is the lower back twist: hold gentle stretch for up to 20 seconds each side.

7. Deep knee bends

These strain the knee ligaments and cartilages.

Danger (Figure 3.19 (a))

Safer alternative (Figure 3.19 (b))

Half or quarter squats – keep knees in line with feet (do not go lower than 90°)

8. Standing side-bend

This puts considerable strain on the spine.

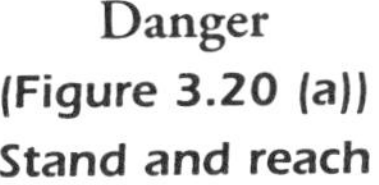

Danger
(Figure 3.20 (a))
Stand and reach

Safer alternative
(Figure 3.20 (b))

There are also exercises which can cause problems if they are performed with poor technique, as follows.

1. Push-ups or press-ups

These must be carried out with a straight body and no 'sag' in the middle. Half press-ups with the knees on the floor are probably better for most people, especially children.

2. Squat thrusts

As with press-ups these must be carried out with a straight body. This is a very demanding exercise and the sagging back which is a common fault is potentially very damaging.

3. Astride jumps

The knees must be directly in line with the feet. Problems occur when the knees are turned inward and landing is on the toes only. Any repeated jumping activity like this has very high 'impact' with resulting potential wear on feet and ankles, knees, hips and back. These jumping exercises need to be treated with great care. Lower impact activities such as skipping can be used instead.

Warm-up bank

Activities for General Mobilising

Individual/creative ideas:

- Shake imaginary pieces of sellotape off your fingers.
- Shoot hands out to pop imaginary bubbles – high, low, forward and sideways.
- Throw an imaginary wellie boot out of sight. Try other imaginary throwing actions if they are known by the children. For example discus, caber, cricket ball, etc.
- Imagine you are walking over a fire ... the ground is very hot ... your feet hardly touch the floor but you must cross the fire (for ankles and feet).
- Imagine you are a cat. When you are angry you arch your back and growl. When you are happy you lower your back, stick your bottom in the air and purr! Put your head down when you are angry and lift it up when you are happy.
- Pretend you are a leaf or a kite caught up in a fierce wind. Spin and twist and bend as you fly around the room. Look out for other leaves !
- Act out your favourite sport – make sure your friends can recognise it.
- Hula Hoops. Try to keep a Hula Hoop spinning around your waist. You must really circle your hips.

Activities in pairs:

'Shadows' (Figure 3.21). Stand one behind the other. One leads, moving from side to side, stretching up arms, lifting legs etc. Partner follows. Change around.

Figure 3.21

Back to back passing (Figure 3.22). Stand back to back. Pass an object (bean bag or ball) from side to side, twisting. Pass the object between the legs and over the head. Repeat the actions on command or in sequence.

Figure 3.22

Back-to-back stretch (Figure 3.23). Stand back to back and link arms. One of you gently bends over so your partner is lying stretched over your back. It is easier (and safer) to do if you are the same height. Change around.

Figure 3.23

Pairs rocking (Figure 3.24). Sit close together with your legs around each other. Rock from side to side slapping your hands on the floor as you change sides. Lean backwards and forwards. Make up your own routine of rocking movements.

Figure 3.24

Hoop Threading (in pairs or in larger groups) (Figure 3.25). See how quickly you can get your partner through a hoop first one way, then the other. Change over. You could include running to a line and back in between the 'threading'.

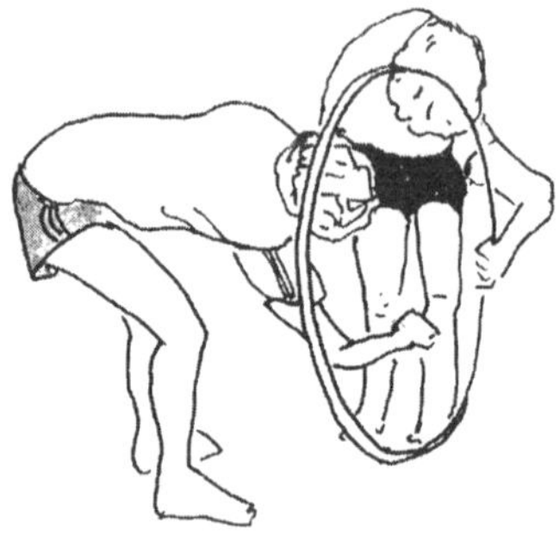

Figure 3.25

Pairs shuttles. Face your partner on opposite lines. Run in to the centre, run around your partner without touching them and run back to your own line. Run in again, leap-frog each other and run back to your own line. Run in, and go under each other's legs,and run back to your own line. Complete this as a race after you have practised each part in turn.

Oranges and Lemons (Figure 3.26). Get in a 'doggie' position on all fours. Your partner must go underneath you without touching you as quickly as they can. Change over. Add relay running in between (to a line and back)

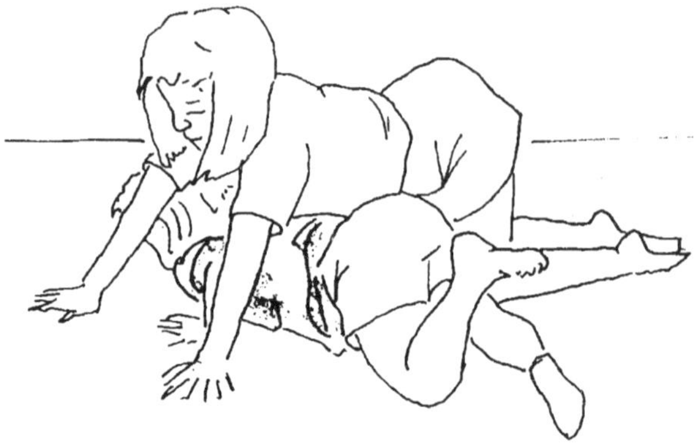

Figure 3.26

Twister (Figure 3.27). Hold hands with your partner. Label yourselves 'A' and 'B'. 'A' steps left leg over right arm, 'B' steps right leg over left arm. From bent position both twist round and step out.

Figure 3.27

Knee touches (Figure 3.28). Hold left hands only with your partner. On 'Go', 'A' tries to touch 'B' as many times as they can on the knees with their right hand in 30 seconds. 'B' must not let them! Do not let go of hands. Change over and 'B' has a chance to beat 'A's' score. The teacher needs to ensure both partners are similar in strength for this activity.

Figure 3.28

Obstacle relays. Run to a given line and back, performing different movements on the way, as set up and directed by the teacher. When one returns the partner goes. This can involve using mats, simple apparatus or small equipment. Suggested movements to include: any roll on a mat, weaving in and out of cones, perform a forward roll on a bar, weave in and out of the frame (through the 'gates'), swinging on a bar, crawling under a bench, going over and under objects (hurdles, or chairs), getting in and out of a hoop, etc.

The Supplenss Bank

This bank includes a selection of warm-up activities which involve stretching and general mobilising of the joints. Some of the activities also include running (stamina), but the main emphasis is on stretching. We have also included a selection of static stretches which are recommended as safe exercises to use with children.

Remember: never bounce when stretching. Stretch slowly and carefully in a controlled way and hold the stretches for 6–10 seconds each. Always repeat stretches.

Basic Stretching Exercises

1. Whole body stretches, sitting, standing and lying down (Figures 3.29–3.32).

These are good for everyone, but particularly appropriate for very young children.

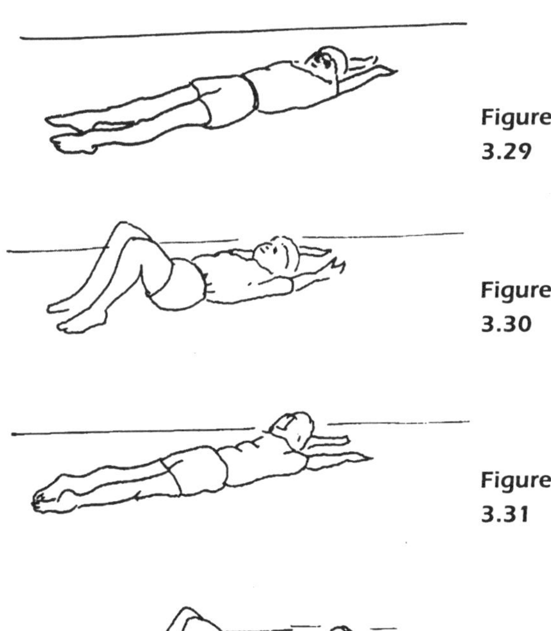

Figure 3.29

Figure 3.30

Figure 3.31

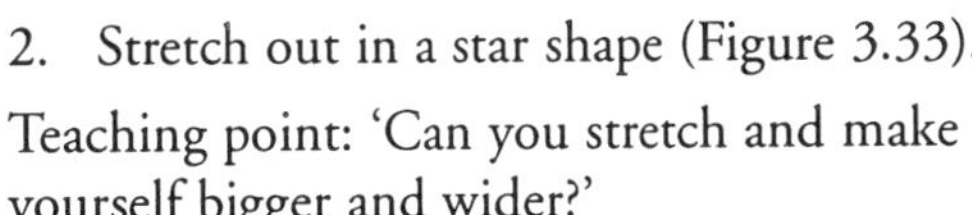

Figure 3.32

2. Stretch out in a star shape (Figure 3.33).

Teaching point: 'Can you stretch and make yourself bigger and wider?'

Figure 3.33

3. Sit on the floor and stretch out your legs wide (Figure 3.34).

Teaching point: 'Can you make your legs straight and sit up tall?'

Figure 3.34

Specific stretches

Do these stretches slowly and in a controlled way. Use some gentle background music.

1. Calf muscles (Figure 3.35).Raise and lower the heel. Check: Both feet facing forwards. Feet apart, back straight.

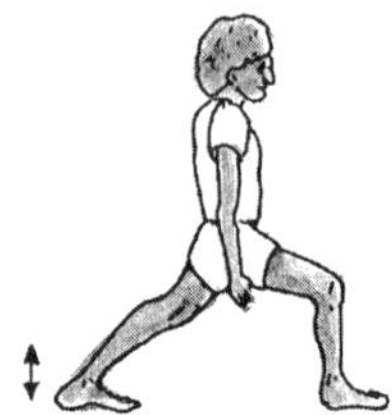

Figure 3.35

2(a). Back of upper leg (hamstrings) (Figure 3.36). On back, legs bent. Ease thigh towards chest. Hold leg below knee.

Check: Back on floor. Do not hold knee joint.

Figure 3.36

2(b). Back of upper leg (hamstrings). Bend front leg, hold ankle. Gently lean back at the hips to straighten leg.

Check: Back leg is bent, back straight.

3. Front of upper leg (quadriceps) (Figure 3.37). Knees close together. Push foot into hand, push hips forward.

Check: Do not push foot into bottom (may cause damage to knee joint).

Figure 3.37

4(a). Inner thigh (groin) (Figure 3.38).

Feet facing forwards. Lean to one side. Keep back straight.

Check: Feet kept flat on floor.

Figure 3.38

4(b). Inner thigh (groin) (Figure 3.39).Sit with feet together. Gently push the knees to the floor.

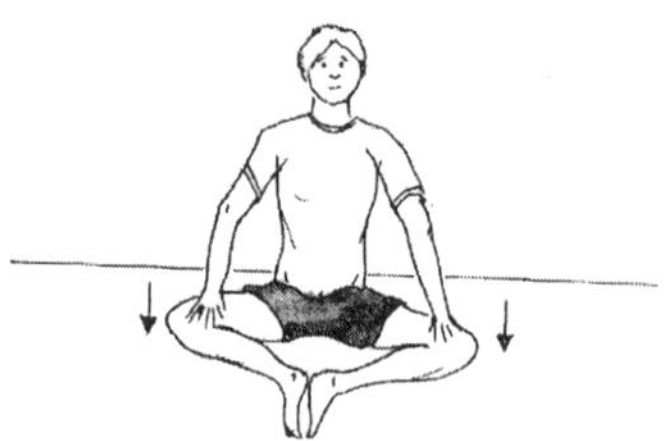

Figure 3.39

5. Hip flexors (Figure 3.40). Feet facing forwards and hips forward. Bend front knee.

Check: Back is straight. Keep heels down.

Figure 3.40

6. Outer thigh (Figure 3.41). Sit and bend one knee up to chest. Put foot across to other side of leg on the floor.

Figure 3.41

7. Side muscles (Figure 3.42). Knees slightly bent. Stretch arms up then lean to one side.

Check: Back is straight. Knees are bent.

Figure 3.42

8(a). Back muscles (Figure 3.43).Sitting, curl the spine taking chin to chest.

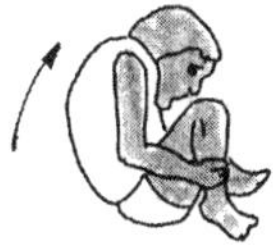

Figure 3.43

8(b). Back muscles (Figure 3.44). On hands and knees. 'Hump' back upwards. Keep head down.

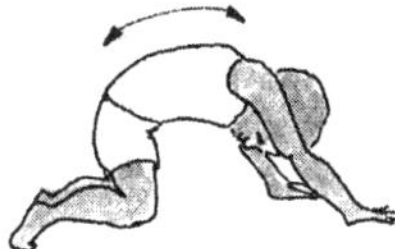

Figure 3.44

9. Arm muscles (back of upper arm) (Figure 3.45). Lift elbow high with hand down back. Push elbow down with other hand

Check: Do not force head forward.

3.45

10. Shoulder muscles (Figure 3.46). Wrap arms round body. 'Hug' tightly.

Check: Back is straight.

Figure 3.46

11. Upper back (Figure 3.47). Link hands behind back. Lift arms up.

Figure 3.47

12. Side leg raises. Lie on side. Lift leg and lower. Change sides.

Check: Do not roll back onto bottom. Keep hips square to the floor.

13. Stomach muscles (Figure 3.48). Lie on tummy. Place palms of hands and lower arms on the floor. Raise head and shoulders.

Figure 3.48(a)

Check: Do not over arch the back.

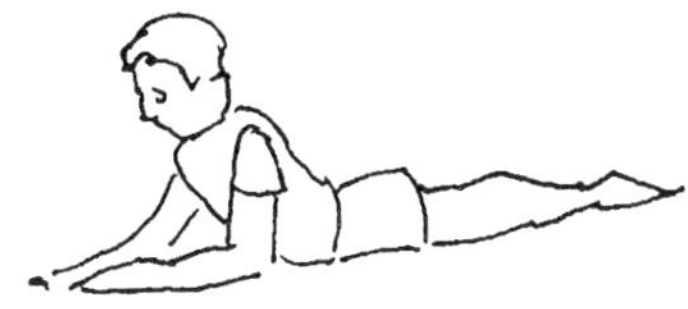

Figure 3.48(b)

Strength Activities

Individual

1. 'Half squats' (leg strength) (Figure 3.49). With the arms folded sit down on a chair and stand alternately. Sit carefully to avoid jarring the lower spine. It is important that the chair is a safe height. The seat should be at knee height. If the chair is lower than this the activity becomes dangerous for the knee joints.

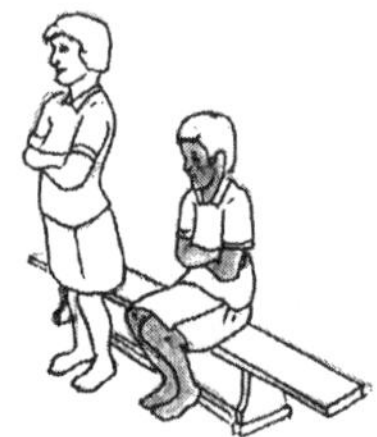

Figure 3.49

2. 'Floor dips' (arm strength) (Figure 3.50). Sit with bent legs. Slowly bend the arms and then straighten them. The arms should not bend beyond a right angle.

Figure 3.50

3. 'Russian kick' (leg strength) (Figure 3.51). Kick the legs up and down alternately while resting on the elbows. Never cycle the legs as this puts strain on the back.

Figure 3.51

4. 'Power pull-ups' (arm strength) (Figure 3.52).Ensure that the bar is absolutely stable. Pull up until the chin touches the bar. Lower carefully. Keep hands apart, body held straight, no sagging in the middle.

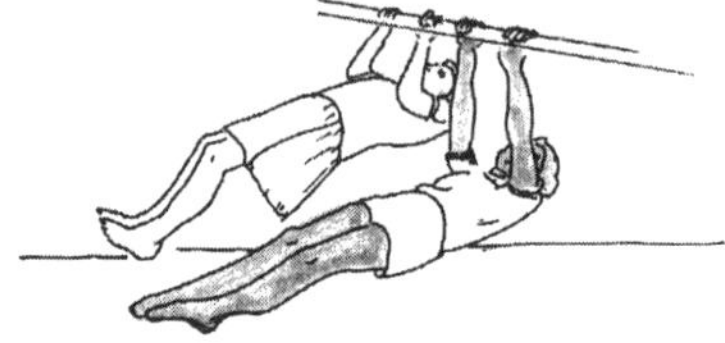

Figure 3.52

5. 'Doggie press-ups' (arm, shoulder and chest strength). Position as in Figure 3.53. Bend the arms until the chin touches the ground and then straighten. Keep the body tense; do not sag in the middle, as this can damage the back.

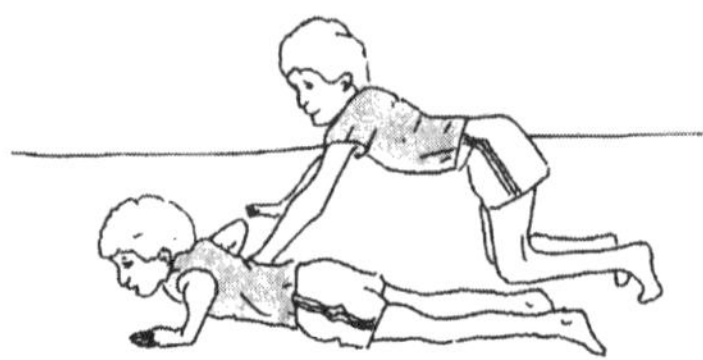

Figure 3.53

6. 'Curl-ups' (stomach muscles) (Figure 3.54). Lie on back with legs bent (not held or put under a bar). Place the arms across the chest, resting on the shoulders. Sit up slowly as far as you can or until the elbows touch the knees. Gently lower to the floor. Alternatively place the palms of the hands on the thighs, and sit up slowly sliding the palms along the legs as far as you can (to the knees if possible). Then lower carefully.

Figure 3.54

7. 'The treadmill' (arm and leg strength) (Figure 3.55). Start with one leg forward with the knee under the chest. Place the hands under the shoulders, fingers pointing forwards. Keep the hips high and the back straight. Reverse the position of the legs, continue rhythmically.

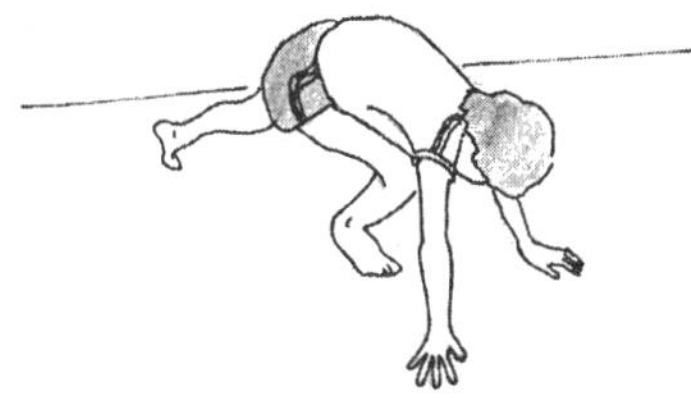

Figure 3.55

8. 'Clockwork' (arm strength) (Figure 3.56). From the front support position, take the feet round in a complete circle, hands turning on the spot. Keep the back straight, and the bottom down. Take regular breaks.

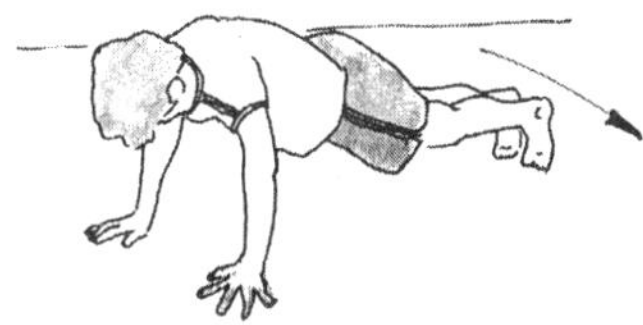

Figure 3.56

9. 'Heel tap' (leg strength) (Figure 3.57). Step and tap the heel behind the leg. Repeat tapping alternate heels. Add a hop to increase the intensity of the activity.

Figure 3.57

10. 'Handstands' (arm and shoulder strength) Place the hands shoulder width apart on the floor. Attempt to kick up into a handstand – weight on hands. Make sure the children look at the floor between their hands all the time. Practise first with little two-footed 'bunny jumps' to build confidence.

Partner/group activities

These partner strength exercises are good fun to do but great care must be taken to ensure they are done sensibly and safely by the class. Warn the children not to try these activities unsupervised (in the playground or at home) as they can be dangerous.

1. 'Slaps' (Figure 3.58). Put the children in pairs of similar size and muscular development. Number them 'A' and 'B'. 'As' hold up their hands and 'Bs' hold them by the wrists. 'As' have to try to touch 'Bs' on the cheeks as often as they can in the time limit (suggested 20–30 seconds). They must not let go of the wrists. 'Bs' attempt to keep the hands away! Change over. Make sure that no one actually slaps their partner!

Figure 3.58

2. 'Partner push'. Two children face each other (again make sure they are of similar build and size). 'A' and 'B' put their hands on each other's shoulders (keeping arms straight). 'B' tries to walk forward and push 'A' backwards. 'A' tries to keep 'B' on the spot. Put a time limit on this activity (suggested 3–5 seconds for each push). Change around and repeat several times each.
3. 'Back to back' (Figure 3.59). The children should be put in pairs with a partner of equal height and size. They sit back to back with their arms linked behind their backs. They try to stand up and sit down in a controlled way, slowly. Emphasise that this is not a race and the activity should be performed on mats. Try some variations – have a bean bag balanced on their heads.

NB. This needs to be done sensibly and with care to avoid undue strains on the knees and other joints.

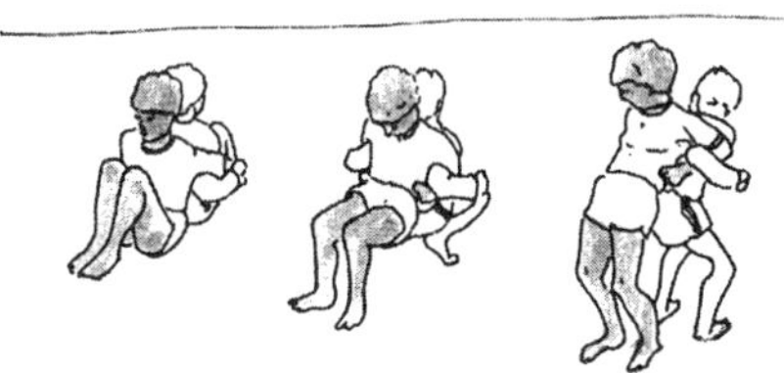

Figure 3.59

4. 'Elbow pull' (Figure 3.60). Partners stand sideways and link arms at the elbow. On a signal they both try to pull their partners back in their direction. Set a time limit (suggested 3–5 seconds). They can then try again with left elbows.

Figure 3.60

5. 'Double leg strength' (Figure 3.61). Partners sit facing each other on a mat. 'A' places his/her feet inside 'B's' feet. On a signal 'A' attempts to push 'B's' legs apart. 'B' tries to keep his or her legs together. Set a time limit of no longer than 10 seconds for each attempt. Change over.

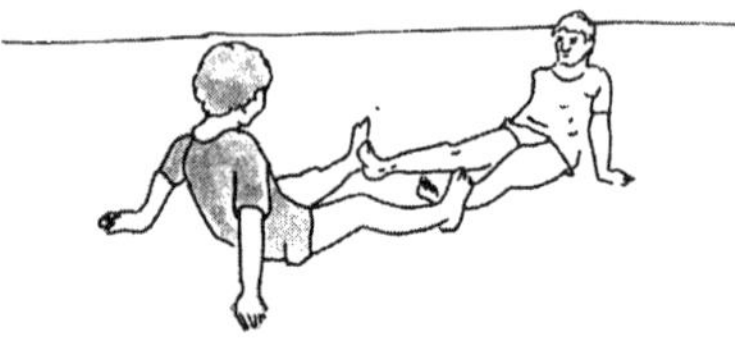

Figure 3.61

6. 'Armclaps' (Figure 3.62). Lie head to head on a mat. 'A' has his or her arms straight, palms facing upwards. 'B' holds 'A's' wrists, knuckles upwards. On a signal 'A' tries to clap their hands over his or her head. 'B' tries to stop them by holding the arms down. Set a time limit of no longer than 10 seconds for each attempt. Change over.

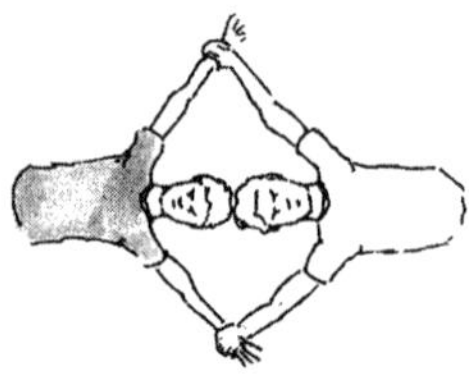

Figure 3.62

7. 'Partner foot clap' (Figure 3.63). Partners sit facing each other, leaning on their hands. They clap their feet together, first the right foot, then the left foot up to a set number (e.g. 15 claps).

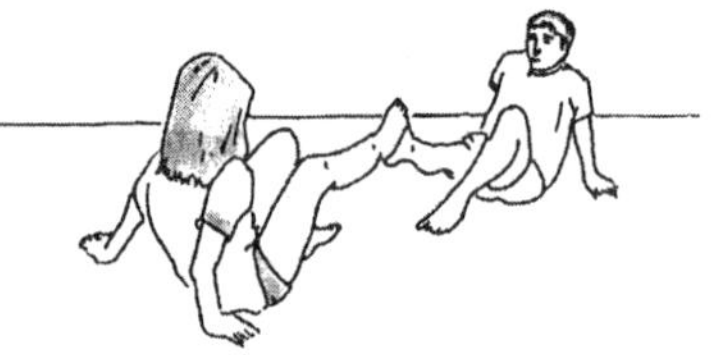

Figure 3.63

8. 'Chinese wrestling' (Figure 3.64). Partners sit back to back and link arms. On a signal they try to tip each other sideways so that their partner's shoulder touches the mat.

Figure 3.64

9. 'Back to back hold' (Figure 3.65). The children try holding the back to back position for a set time (suggested 10 seconds).

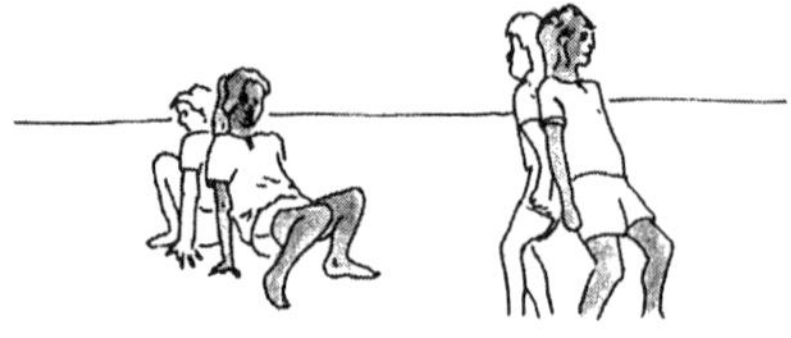

Figure 3.65

10. 'Partner sit-ups' (Figure 3.66). Sit side by side with a partner. Mirror their sit-ups. Stress that the exercise should be completed slowly and properly, and that the quality is more important than the speed.

Remember: Sit-ups should never be completed with the feet held, or with linked hands pulling from behind the head (this can damage the spinal column). Hands should be on the shoulders or resting on the thighs, the knees should be bent throughout the exercise.

Figure 3.66

Group relays

1. 'Press-up relay' (Figure 3.67). Put the children in teams of four or five. The whole team starts in the 'doggie' press-up position. The end person crawls under the rest of the team, runs around a marker and joins the end of the line in the 'doggie' position. Repeat until all the team have had a go. You could use the same idea but with the team in a full press-up position as another activity.

Figure 3.67

2. Back to back (Figure 3.68). Five or six children sit in a circle, backs facing inwards, arms linked. They all push backwards and try to stand up.

Figure 3.68

3. Roll the ball and push up (Figure 3.69). A ball is rolled under the group, the children then perform a small number of press-ups (1, 2 or 3). The group should have completed their press-ups before the ball is returned overhead by the thrower.

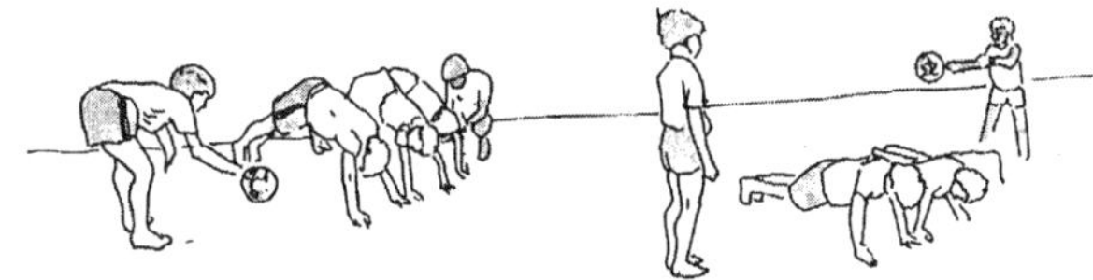

Figure 3.69

Stamina/General Warming up Activities

All these activities are suitable for a large space indoors or outdoors and involve the whole class. Minimum or no apparatus is required. The warm-ups take varying amounts of time to complete, but the organisation of each activity will speed up the more times they are repeated.

Individual

1. Random jogging around the space ... change directions, go forwards, backwards and sideways (Figure 3.70). Vary the length of each stride and also the speed at which the children travel. Stop and go on command.

Figure 3.70

2. 'North', 'South', 'East' and 'West' (Figure 3.71). Pupils run to each direction on command. You can give the pupils numbers, calling number 1's to the East, number 4's South ... and 'all change' where they all change direction. Remind the children to look out for others when they are running at random. There are many variations to this game. You can use railway stations as names, parts of the world, whatever is relevant to a topic you may be covering in class at the time.

Figure 3.71

3. 'Ships' (Figure 3.72). The children skip around as if they are on board a ship at sea. Call out instructions and the children must follow your orders: 'Scrub the deck'... 'pull in the mainsail' ... 'climb the rigging'... 'dance to the hornpipe' ... 'captains coming' (salute and march) ... and finally abandon ship!

Figure 3.72

4. 'Shapes' (Figure 3.73). The children jog out shapes on the ground with their pathways. Square, circle, star, triangle etc. Alternatively they can 'write' their names on the ground with their feet. Encourage the children to move forwards, backwards and sideways, changing the sizes of the steps.

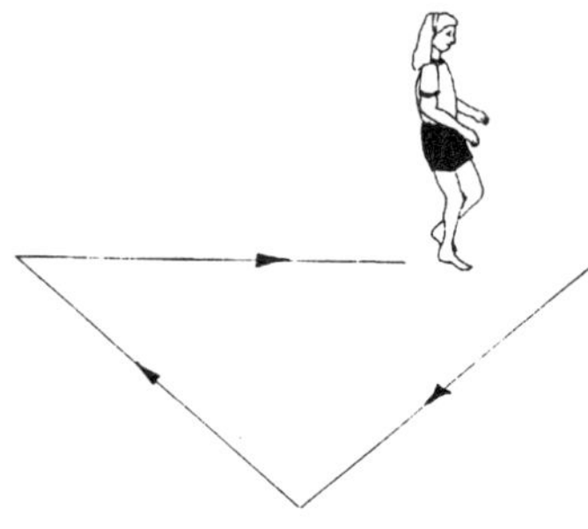

Figure 3.73

5. Run in a variety of different styles, pumping arms, lifting the knees high etc. Run in the style of a hurdler, a boxer, a long distance runner etc. Ask the children to make up their own 'styles'.

6 'Beans' (Figure 3.74). Call out the names of different types of beans. The children must perform an action associated with the bean! For example:

- *Runner beans* – jog.
- *Broad beans* – make a wide shape.
- *Jelly beans* – shake all over.
- *Frozen beans* – stand still ... freeze!
- *Chilli beans* – shake your limbs.
- *Beans on toast* – stretch out on a mat.

Figure 3.74

7. Jogging ... when the children meet a line they perform five jumps over the line, then continue to jog (Figure 3.75). Repeat with cross-steps over a line, or any other jumping/stepping action you like. Get the children to think up some of their own.

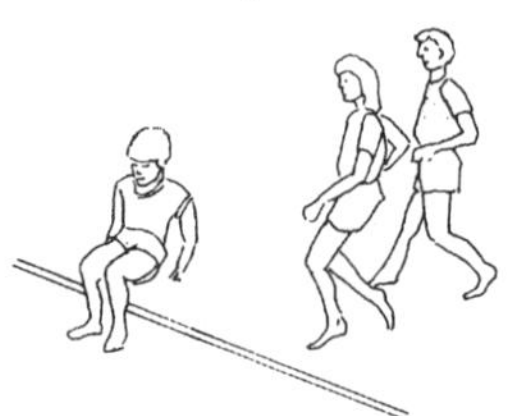

Figure 3.75

8. 'Friends' (Figure 3.76). Jog in and out of spaces. When the children meet someone else they should stop and slap hands, then continue to jog. Progress by jumping to slap hands in the air – 'high fives'. American Basketball style! Ask the children to think of their own active greetings.

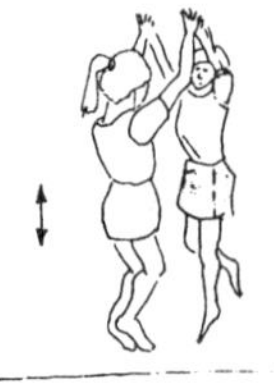

Figure 3.76

9. Line relays (Figure 3.77). Run to a set line, perform a small number of repetitions of a given exercise and return to the starting line each time. Suggested exercises:

- star jumps
- press-ups
- squat jumps (not too low)
- sit-ups (knees bent, hands on shoulders or ears, not linked behind head)

Figure 3.77

10. Copy the movements of objects such as trains, aeroplanes, kites, etc. Alternatively copy animals and birds: 'Stretch like a cat', 'move like a frog', 'spring like a kangaroo', 'move sideways like a crab', 'soar like a bird' etc.

Remember: limit the amount of time on an exercise that puts pressure on a particular joint.

11. 'Here, there and everywhere' (Figure 3.78). Label three areas of the room or playground 'here', 'there' and the central space 'everywhere'. The children must run to the area called out by the teacher. The last child to get to the area is out (give them some chances to start with!). Point in the direction of the space. The children become very confused as the words are similar. Start to confuse them further by trying to catch them out. Point to one space and call out another. Any child who goes the wrong way is also out. When there are 5 or 6 children left, have a straight race to one area to decide the winner... then repeat the game. Don't leave children 'out' for more than a short time.

Figure 3.78

12. Skipping (Figure 3.79). Each child should have a rope. Try some 'tricks' with the ropes ... one foot, loop the rope, skiing action, leg swings from side to side whilst skipping etc. Ask the children to make up their own 'tricks'. They can also try skipping with two people using one rope – this is great fun and hard work.

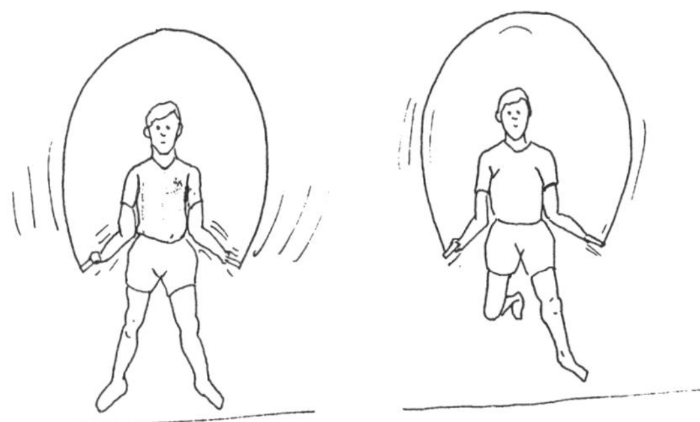

Figure 3.79

13. Short runs ... how far can the children travel in a certain length of time (between 5 and 10 seconds)? Repeat this with crawling, skipping, travelling on hands and feet etc. See if the same children can improve when they try again.

14. '*Winnie the Pooh*' (Figure 3.80). The children run around keeping in spaces and looking out for others. The teacher calls out a character from '*Winnie the Pooh*'. The children travel in this way until you call out a new character. Use 'Pooh' as a chance to give the class a brief rest!

- *Tigger* – leaps ... 1 foot to the other.
- *Roo* – bouncing ... 2 feet to 2 feet
- *Rabbit* – hopping ... 1 foot to the same foot
- *Piglet* – hopscotch
- *Pooh* – stop still...freeze.

Figure 3.80

15. 'Reverse instructions'. Children skip in and out stopping and starting on command. Skip equals stop, and stop equals skip! Try this with leaping, jumping, jogging and hopping reversing the commands. The children must really concentrate on your instructions and listen.

16. 'Card game' (Figure 3.81). Put out four cones in the corners of the room or space. Each must have a different symbol from a pack of playing cards (heart, club, etc.) attached to it so it can be seen at a distance. Alternatively you can put the symbol on a card and pin it on the wall with a cone nearby. Place a pack of cards in the centre of the room. The children pick up a card and must jog the number of times on the card around the cone and back to the centre. When they have completed this, they return the old card and pick up a new one. A picture card is five circuits around the whole square. This is a good warm-up with some music in the background.

You can vary this warm-up by having extra cards at each cone stating a specific exercise. For example, ♥ = sit ups, ♦ = star jumps, ♠ = press ups, ♣ = skip. The children go to the cone and perform the number of repetitions of the exercise, as stated on the card, e.g. 6 = 6 sit-ups. They then return the card and collect a new one.

Figure 3.81

17. Run for 10 paces, then include a whole body stretch, five waist twists, then run 20 paces, etc. Build this up to include a variety of whole body stretches interspersed with running.

18. Aerobics (Figure 3.82). Using some 'beaty' music, get the children bouncing on two feet in time with the music. Put in some simple arm actions (e.g. bending and extending the arms out to the side). Change the action to skiing (two feet jumping from side to side, using the arms to get rhythm). Then skip from side to side on the spot (again get the children to use their arms).

Other examples of simple actions you could include are 'bottom kicks', leg swings from side to side, cross steps, high knees (as if you are running on the spot) etc. The children love to 'dance' so get them to think up their own exercises.

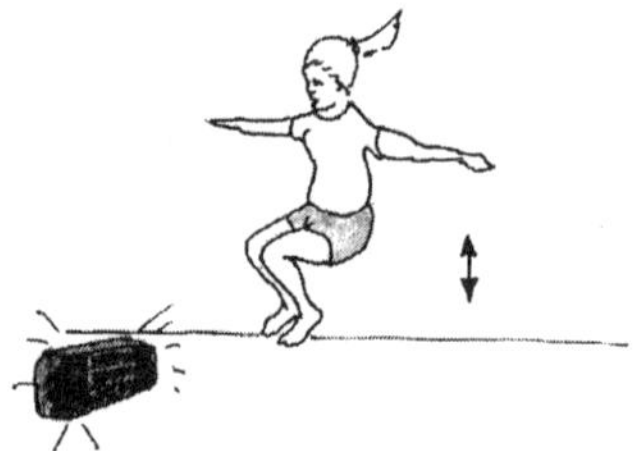

Figure 3.82

19. 'Islands' (Figure 3.83). Use mats or hoops to represent 'home'. The children travel around the space as directed by the teacher in a variety of ways... jogging, hopping, skipping etc. When the teacher calls 'home' they must sprint back to their 'home' and sit down. Repeat several times. This can be varied by giving each 'home' a different name.

Figure 3.83

20. Number the class from 1 to 5. They run in and out of spaces, looking out for others. The teacher calls a number and this group must run into the centre of the area and perform some stretching exercises. When this group have completed the stretches call in a different group (by number). Make sure that each of the groups has the same number of exercises in the centre.

21. Use the corners of any court markings on the floor. Ask the class to touch the corners and return to a space. Split the class into 4–6 teams. Each team 'owns' a basket of balls, hoops, beanbags, etc. (Figure 3.84). On 'go' the teams have to collect as many items as they can from other group's baskets. They may only collect one at a time. Teams may not defend their own basket!

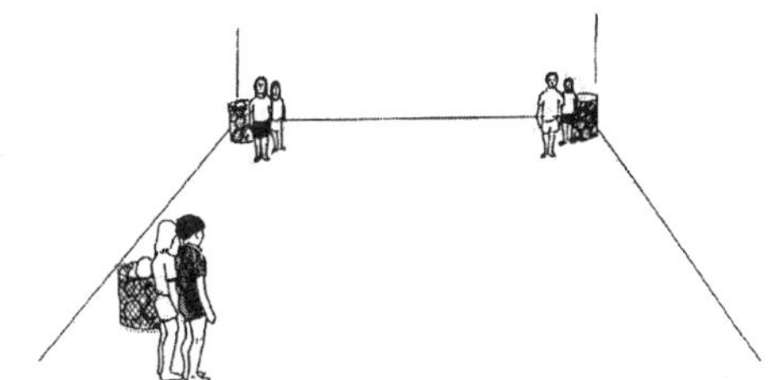

Figure 3.84

22. In a similar game to the above, one or two children are in charge of a basket of hoops, beanbags or balls. The team must start alongside the basket. On 'GO' the two children throw out the contents of the basket one item at a time. The other pupils must retrieve them individually, as quickly as possible, returning the items to the basket.

    The object of the game is to see if the 'throwers' can beat the 'collectors'. You can have several baskets working at the same time, but care must be taken with the type of objects ... remember they will be thrown out, and other children may be in the way.

23. Activity circuits (Figure 3.85). These need some preparation, but can work very well and can be an enjoyable way of practising a variety of skills. Put a number of stations around the

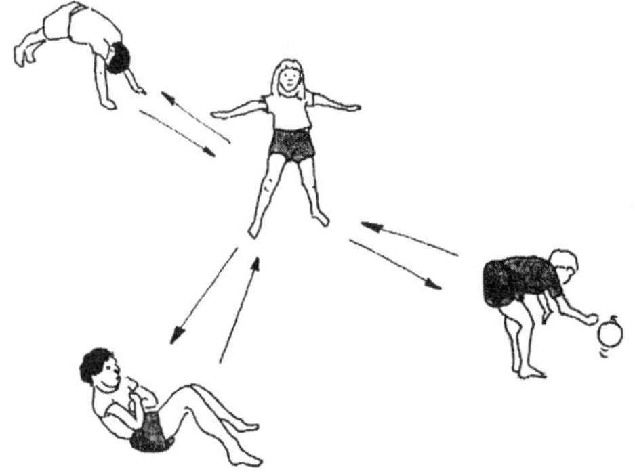

Figure 3.85

    area, where either a skill (throwing/catching) or an exercise (sit-ups, star jumps) must be performed. It is a good idea to use large activity cards at each station (once made you always have them as a resource).

You can vary this by timing a minute at each station, and then getting the children into the centre of the room to perform some 'aerobics', stretching exercises, or fitness exercises, as directed by you. Then send them out to the next skill/station.

'Tag' games

These tend to involve a lot of running and so, if well managed, are effective in getting children 'warm' quickly, and if reasonably prolonged will help develop children's stamina.

1. 'Stuck in the mud' (Figure 3.86). Three or four children are 'up' or 'it' and have bands to distinguish them from the rest of the class. When they catch someone, the caught child must stand with their arms stretched out until they are released. This can be done in a variety of ways ...crawling under the legs, going under one arm, etc. Change the children who are 'up' every 2–3 minutes.

Figure 3.86

2. 'Tag tails'. All children have a band or bib tucked into their shorts or skirts at the back. The children who are 'up' must try to take their 'tails' and collect as many as they can. You can play this as a competition: the catchers must collect as many 'tails' as they can. Alternatively the tagged pupils can put on their bibs when caught and become extra catchers until the whole class is caught.

3. 'Hospital tag'. Three or four children are 'up'. They have one hand on their heads. When they catch another child this child joins them as another catcher with one hand holding the part of the body he or she was tagged! Continue until the whole class is caught.

4. 'Chain tag'. Two or three pairs are 'up'. They hold hands and must tag others while still joined together. Tagged children join onto the chain. When the chain becomes four children, it must split up to form two new pairs.

Pairs Activities

1. 'Rats and Rabbits' (Figure 3.87). 'A' stands on a line with their back to 'B'. 'B' creeps up and touches 'A' on the shoulder. 'A' can then turn and chase 'B' back to his or her starting line. If 'A' catches 'B' before he or she reaches the line 'A' gets a point, and if 'B' manages to get to the line first then they get the point. Repeat several times and then change the children over.

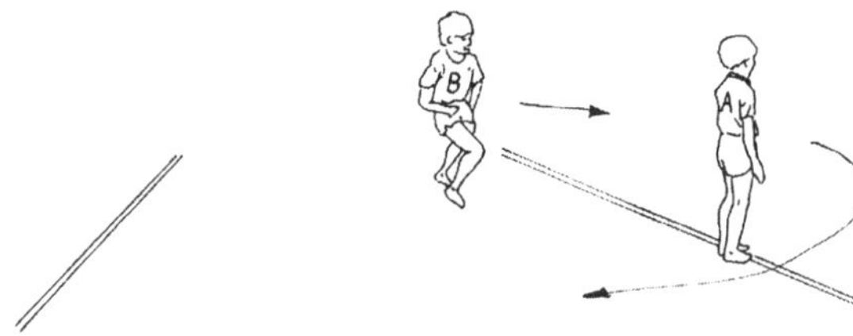

Figure 3.87

2. Pairs relays. Run as a relay (one after the other) to a designated line and back. Change the races ... skipping, sidesteps, hands and feet, etc. Try putting in exercises on the line as well ... star jumps, press-ups, etc. You could also use equipment; for example: bounce a ball, roll a ball, dribble a ball, etc.

3. 'Fetch and carry'. Each child will need a bean bag or ball (any size). One ball or bean bag is placed on a line away from the starting (or base-) line. The children start together on the start line, 'A' with the second ball or bean-bag. 'A' must run out and put the bean-bag or ball on the far line. 'B' must collect them and bring them back to the base line. They continue to do this until eventually one will catch up the other (either 'A' will not have a ball or bean bag to put out, or 'B' will not have one to collect!) This then gives you a winner!

4. 'Shadows'. Follow a partner around, copying their every movement. Children try to lose their partners by changing speeds and directions. Use a whistle for them to freeze and see if they have successfully lost their shadows. If they can touch each other with an outstretched arm then they have not been successful! Change over, have several attempts each.

5. Pairs shuttles. The children face each other on opposite lines (Figure 3.88). They run in, circle their partner without touching them and sprint back to their line (the line they started on). On touching their line they run in again and leap frog each other before returning to their line. They run in a third time and must go under each other's legs before returning to the line. This series can be repeated several times as a race. It is a good idea to get the class to practise each part in turn before they do this!

Figure 3.88

Group activities

1. 'Continuous relays' (Figure 3.89). Number the class 1 to 4. Stand each group in a corner of the working space in a relay line facing inwards. The children run in order across the room to join the back of the line diagonally opposite. This is a continuous running activity. You can stop the activity when everyone has returned to their original place.

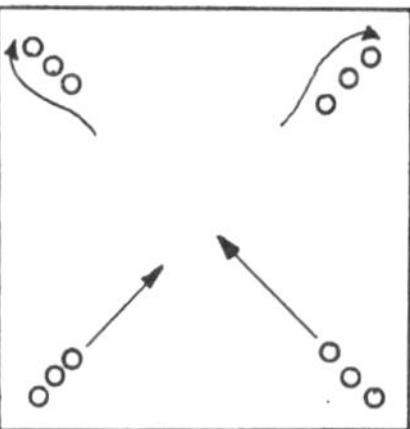

Figure 3.89

2. 'Cat and mouse' (Figure 3.90). The children sit in pairs, one behind the other, spread randomly around the space. Choose a pair to be 'up'. One is the 'cat' and the other the 'mouse'. On the word 'go', the cat chases the mouse in and out of the children sitting on the floor. If the 'cat' catches the 'mouse', they immediately change roles. The ' mouse' can sit down behind any pair of children sitting on the floor when they are tired. The child in the front then becomes the new 'mouse' and has to get up and start running immediately without being caught by the cat! Introduce

several more 'cats' and 'mice'. The 'cats' are only allowed to chase their own 'mice' (otherwise it becomes too confusing for the poor 'mice').

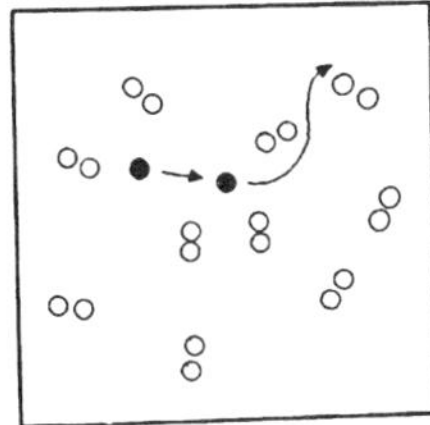

Figure 3.90

3. 'Groups'. The children jog in and out, moving freely around the space. Encourage them to run in all directions and not simply in circles, looking out for others as they jog. Call out a number. The children have to get into a group of this size as quickly as they can and sit down. The children not in the correct sized group collect a penalty (or they can be 'out'). Continue, calling other numbers. The smaller the number the easier it is for the children. Try some large numbers, or insist the groups are of mixed sexes! Give all the children with penalties a 'fun' forfeit at the end of the game.

4. 'Beat the passes' (Figure 3.91). This warm-up can be used with any even-sized group. Six or eight children in a group is ideal. Divide the children into two halves (e.g. with a group of six, two smaller groups of three). One group runs in turn to a nominated line and back. Whilst they are the running the other group (in this case three), pass a ball in a triangle, counting the number of successful passes as they go, out loud. When the last runner returns, they shout 'stop' and the throwers stop counting. The groups change over and the new throwers try to get more passes than the first group to be the winners. You can use any skill for the activity – football passes, throwing a rugby ball etc. You can also ask the runners to go twice each to give the throwers more time. Adapt it however you like (e.g. the runners use skipping ropes, or complete exercises). The children love the competitive element of this activity.

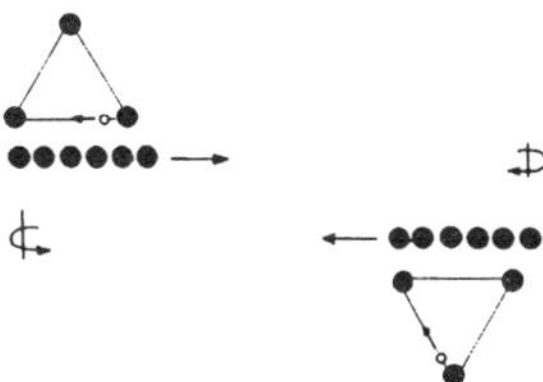

Figure 3.91

5. 'Circle dodge ball' (Figure 3.92). Divide the class in half. Half the class stand in a circle, with the other half around the edge with a number of foam (or soft) balls. Set a time limit (e.g. 1–2 minutes). The children on the outside throw the balls at the children in the centre, aiming to hit them below the knees. Change the children around at the end of the time. The group which received the fewest hits is the winner.

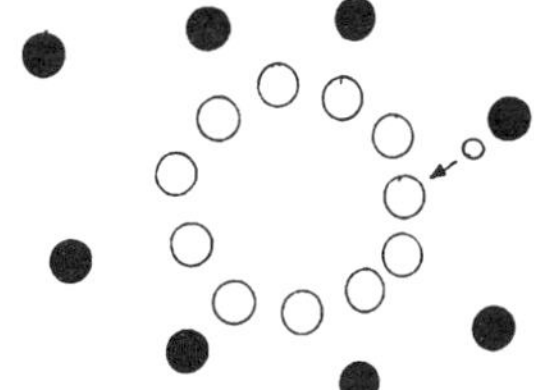

Figure 3.92

6. 'Hoop relay' (Figure 3.93). Put the children into teams, with half on one side and half on the other (for maximum involvement). The children step from hoop to hoop as a relay race, 'tagging' the next child to go. Change to hopping on one foot, or two footed jumping.

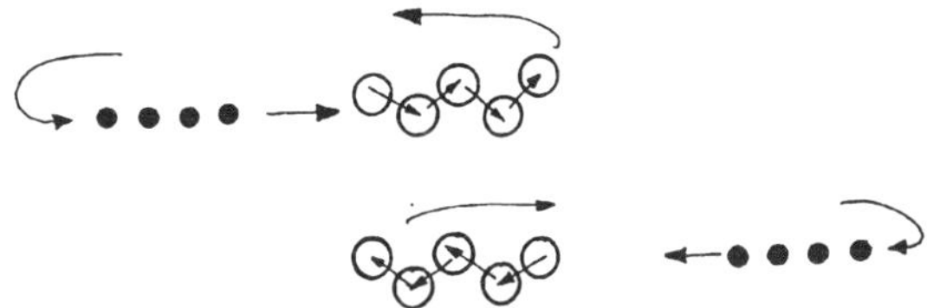

Figure 3.93

7. 'Circle Chase' (Figure 3.94). The class forms a large circle. Number the children 1 to 5. Call out a number. The children with this number run clockwise around the outside of the circle until they get back to their original place. They try to catch the child in front, and try to avoid being caught by the child behind. You could award penalities for all children who get caught, and give them a forfeit at the end of the activity. To involve more children running, you could put the children into several smaller

circles, with numbers 1 to 3 instead. If you do this, you must stress that the children only run around their own circle,otherwise they tend to run all over the place!

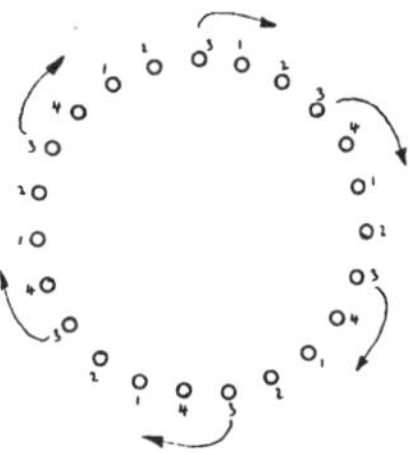

Figure 3.94

Cooling down and relaxation

Why cool down?

Cooling down and relaxing at the end of a period of exercise are important for two main reasons:

1. Much of the activity during the PE lesson has the effect of making children excited. Quite often they will be striving to perform as well as they can whether it is in terms of distance jumped or thrown, speed, quality of movement or keeping going when it would be easier to stop. They may not only be 'wound-up' physically but excited and possibly tense psychologically. A cool-down period not only allows children to unwind and become calm again but assists the effective transition back to classroom learning after the physically active session. It is also important for the children to have time for reflection about what has been achieved and learned and what might need to be done next time. This short, reflective time is a part of the enjoyment of exercise and it is important that it is not lost in the need to change quickly or the bustle of putting away apparatus. It also has an important function in reinforcing in children's minds that PE is about learning and not just about occasional periods of aimless (even if enjoyable) exercise.
2. Cooling down has important physical functions. Probably almost everyone can remember times when we have had to sit through uncomfortable sessions with clothes sticking to our bodies in the classroom (or office) because there wasn't time to shower or cool down properly after exercise. Unfortunately very few primary schools have showers anyway but it is still necessary to ensure that children cool down gradually after strenuous exercise. This is not just for reasons of comfort. Our bodies need to be allowed to return gradually to the resting state just as much as they need to warm up gradually before strenuous exercise. All of the physiological changes that take place in exercise need time to be reversed. During exercise the heart rate and breathing rate are raised sometimes to high levels. The body temperature is raised and there will be sweating – often profuse. There will be changes in the circulation of blood with large amounts being 'shunted' to working areas such as the leg muscles and away from the non-working areas such as the digestive system. If the exercise is very strenuous (such as in running for a sustained period or repeated efforts) there will be waste products in the blood which need to be dispersed. These are the substances which make your limbs feel heavy as you get tired (for example, walking to the top of a steep hill).

In general the cool-down period should do four things:

1. Allow the body (and mind) to return gradually to the non-exercising state (i.e. normal breathing rate and heart rate, normal body temperature, calm mind).
2. Allow the excitement which can accompany exercise to dissipate, together with any physical tension associated with the effort of exercise.
3. Help the circulatory system to ensure adequate return of the blood through the veins to enable the chambers of the heart to refill properly. In gentle rhythmic exercise such as walking following the strenuous part of the lesson, the muscles in the legs literally squeeze or massage the veins to help in returning blood towards the heart. This helps people who have been exercising strenuously to recover more quickly.
4. Help the circulatory system to keep blood flowing through the muscles which have been working hard. This helps to ensure that the waste products of strenuous exercise are dispersed and helps to prevent sore muscles later.

The cool-down period should last from 5 to 10 minutes which, followed by changing (after a wash or shower if possible), should enable children to go on to the next activity, whether in the classroom or not, refreshed, relaxed and composed. Activities appropriate for the cool-down are:

- Gentle jogging, walking or skipping to help promote venous return of the blood (see above) after strenuous exercise.
- Gentle stretching exercises to lengthen muscles which have been involved in vigorous contraction. This also helps to maintain flexibility and prevent muscle soreness.
- Rhythmic flowing loosening or mobiity exercises such as arm swings, reaching to the front or side, leg swings, knee bends, etc. These also help to promote venous return and also help to reduce tension in muscles and joints.
- Specific relaxation exercises such as lying or sitting gently tensing and relaxing each muscle group in turn while focusing on slow, deep and gentle breathing. Children can quite easily learn simple techniques of progressive muscular relaxation or autogenics. Learning to be aware of tension and knowing how to disperse it is particularly important. Learning effective breathing using the diaphragm is important for people of all ages and is helpful in combating stress.

Cool-down bank

All cool-down activities should be performed in a quiet, relaxed and calm way. Use your voice to help create the right atmosphere at the end of the lesson.

1. 'Positive reflections'. Ask all the children to stand still (or lie down on the floor).

   Ask them to think about the lesson and how they have performed:

- How could they have improved their game ?
- What did they like best?
- Which parts of the body benefited best from the lesson?

2. 'Rag doll'. Ask the children to imagine they are a rag doll or a toy soldier. They must imagine that they are getting tired. Their bodies begin to go saggy, and they start to droop. Gradually they begin to crumble to the ground, and eventually become lifeless and still. Talk them through the relaxation slowly, taking each limb in turn. Use your voice in a quiet way.

3. 'Sleeping tigers'. Ask the children to lie on the floor with their eyes closed. Go around the room talking quietly to the class about the lesson. After a few minutes talk, tell the class that when you touch them they can open their eyes and walk slowly and quietly out of the room.

4. 'Relaxed bodies' (Figure 3.95). Ask the children to lie on the floor with their eyes closed. Tell them that every part of their bodies must be relaxed and floppy. To test this you walk around the room lifting up an arm or a leg. When you let it go, it should flop back onto the floor ! You can ask one or two sensible children to help you check that everyone is relaxed.

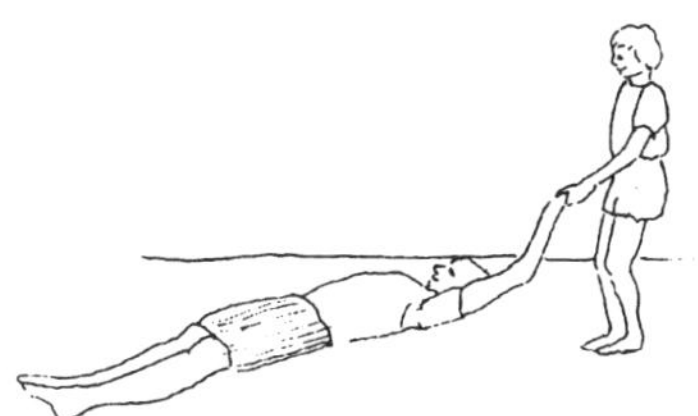

Figure 3.95

5. Muscle relaxation.Ask the children to lie on the floor and relax, closing their eyes. Ask them to breathe slowly, and listen to their heart beat. Slowly tense up the muscles in the feet, breathe out slowly and then relax them again. Repeat this with other muscles in the body.

6. 'Balance' (Figure 3.96). Ask the children to choose a simple balance (not too difficult or strenuous)and to hold it for 10 seconds, then relax. Choose a new balance and repeat (depending on the time left). Alternatively ask the children to choose three different balances and to move slowly from one to the other.

Figure 3.96

7. ‘Sinking feeling’ (Figure 3.97). Ask the children to stand on tip toes and reach to the sky. Gradually sink down into a small ball . . . hold the curled shape for 10 seconds and then relax.

Figure 3.97

8. ‘Ice’! Ask the children to imagine that the floor has been covered with a film of ice. They have to get to the door or the edge without falling over . . . go carefully!!

9. ‘Journey’ (Figure 3.98). Ask the children to lie on their backs and close their eyes. Ask them to think of their journey to school . . . think about what they pass on the way . . . shops?. . . trees ? Talk them into school, through the gate and into the buildings. Use your voice in a very quiet, soothing way.

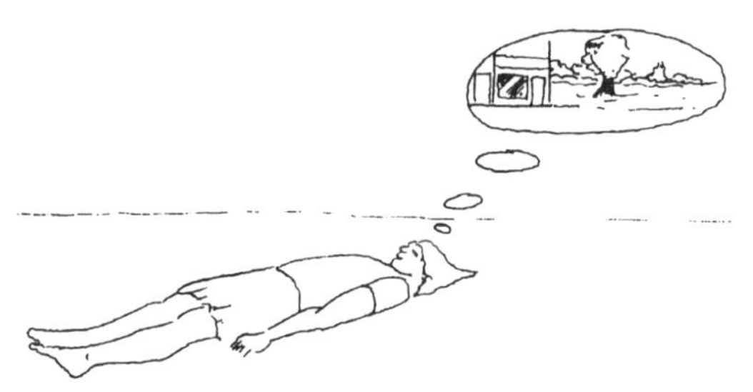

Figure 3.98

10. ‘Slowing up’. Get the children to imagine they are objects slowing down . . . for example . . . imagine they are a train coming into the station . . . a balloon landing on the ground, etc.

11. Repeat suitable movements or skills used in the lesson. Perform them as slowly as possible, taking care to complete the movement or skill properly.

12. ‘Stretches’ (Figures 3.29–3.32, page 23). Go through some stretches, holding each one gently for a long period of time (15 + seconds each). If you have been doing a lot of running activities make sure that you get the children to stretch out the major leg muscles (see the suppleness bank for safe stretches).

13. Give each pupil a large ball. Ask them to keep it moving but they must keep it in contact with the body at all times (Figure 3.99). This activity is also good for ball familiarity.

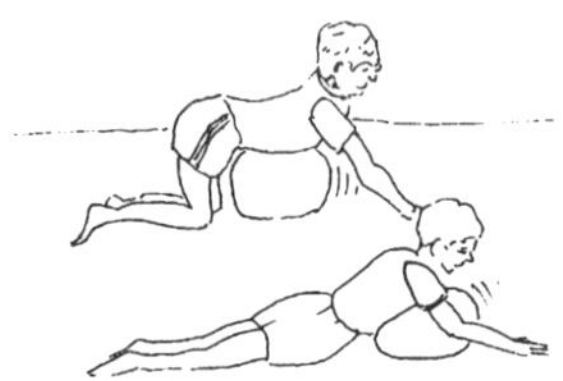

Figure 3.99

14. ‘Music’. Cool-downs provide an excellent opportunity to use atmospheric music . . . ask the children to interpret slow passages . . . the swishing of waves . . . the wind . . . etc. Ask them to ‘act out’ what the music suggests to them.

4 Where to Start

Taking stock

We said at the beginning that it would be helpful to take stock of the situation in your school before deciding exactly what kinds of development are going to be possible. There is nothing to stop you using the lessons in this short guide as they stand (Chapter 5). You can take these lessons as starting points and build up units of work in the six areas of PE focusing on health and fitness as you think appropriate. But we are convinced that to teach about health and fitness effectively you have to give some thought not only to the lessons you plan but to the wider context in which the children are learning. If you are serious about doing that, this chapter is intended to help you by suggesting some questions you might find it helpful to ask, as well as offering a few ideas for addressing some of the issues that arise in many schools. We have tried to put these questions in order; with the issues to do with policy and the status of PE in a school first and the more straightforward practical questions later.

Obviously it isn't possible to provide detailed solutions to practical problems in individual schools but we have tried to suggest the kinds of discussion you may need to have to establish a more effective context for teaching about health and fitness. In a way, what we are trying to do here is to examine the extent to which a school is a 'health-promoting school'. This concerns the ways in which all the aspects of education about health are drawn together in a coherent, planned way. There should be appropriate work on growth and development, relationships and sex, healthy eating, avoiding substance misuse (alcohol, solvents, smoking and other drugs), keeping safe in the home and on the road, as well as physical activity, exercise and rest. A health-promoting school also examines the many factors likely to influence the effectiveness of its teaching about health. One of these factors is the match between the messages taught in lessons and the unconscious messages given out through other aspects of school life.

What is the attitude of the Head? The Head and senior staff, and increasingly the governors, have central roles in setting the direction for the school. These key decision-makers must be well briefed about health and exercise. If you feel there is a lack of information, someone in the school needs to gather together some authoritative and clear documentation. This can be used to support effective arguments for a greater emphasis on physical activity and exercise for all pupils and to promote a greater whole school concern for higher quality teaching. For example the Fitness and Health Advisory Group (HEA/Sports Council) position statement on Children, Exercise and Health should be in every school in the UK. If another copy is needed you can get one from the HEA in London. Other useful references can be found on page 103.

Is there a PE policy or school curriculum statement? This is a basic question which will indicate if PE has appropriate status in a school. There are obviously related questions such as: is PE featured on the school development plan (SDP)? Since the National Curriculum in PE was introduced by law for pupils in Year 1 and Year 3 (and Year 7) in 1992, it seems reasonable to suggest that PE should already have featured on school development plans.

Planning and assessment

PE (and music and art) will not have statutory end-of-key-stage assessment in the form of standard assessment tasks (or SATS). We hope that schools will still take the opportunity when they can to have whole staff discussions about what PE (and music and art) should be like. The discussion should include what kinds of activities children need to experience and what we expect children to know and be able to do. Assessment will be limited to teacher assessment according to general End of Key Stage Descriptions. This means we have, in PE, art and music, the luxury of much more flexibility than in the core subjects. A helpful first step is to draft a PE policy or curriculum statement which takes into account children's needs as well as the requirements of the National Curriculum. There is considerable help with drafting a curriculum statement for PE in the Non-Statutory Guidance. A statement should cover each key stage, use the End of Key Stage Descriptions, define the activities to be covered and the weighting on each one. It should indicate the scope for pupils' choice, the resource implications, general approaches for assessment, record keeping and reporting. It should also be regularly reviewed.

Does the quality of weekly and daily planning for PE in your school compare with the quality of planning for say, English or maths? If planning is less effective in PE than in academic subjects, is it partly because planning for the core subjects is linked to record keeping and assessment and teachers' knowledge of the progress and attainment of individual pupils and groups? In other subjects is it clearer what you expect the children to learn and be able to do? This is the case in many schools and there is a lot of room for improvement in planning and record keeping for PE. We should know what individual children can do and what they should be working on within the context of a progressive scheme of work. Activities from our own experience can be a useful resource to draw on in developing schemes of work but only if they are appropriate for the children we are teaching. So schools need to discuss what children should be doing and learning in PE from the early years to the end of Year 6. This will take some time and may well require specialist support from outside the school. But it is an important step if a school is to develop a PE programme to meet the needs of all children. Planning a programme that is 'owned' by a whole staff group can be a very powerful way of transforming the quality of PE for the pupils. The framework for planning set out in the published programmes of study and end of key stage descriptions in the National Curriculum is general and lacking in detail but it does provide a starting point which teachers can use. The Non-statutory Guidance is much more helpful in this respect.

Effective planning needs to be on three levels in addition to the curriculum statement – i.e. schemes of work, units of work and individual lessons. Schemes of work will cover a whole key stage and include a rationale explaining the reasons for choosing areas of activity to be covered with particular groups of pupils, at particular times, in particular ways. Schemes should include content which pupils will experience, the sequencing of the work, teaching strategies and techniques, organisation, resources needed, how to differentiate to meet the needs of all pupils, and references to how assessment and record keeping will be done. The Non-Statutory Guidance provides clear help about drafting schemes of work for PE. Planning at this level in PE is still new for many primary schools, but it is a worthwhile challenge.

Planning for individual lessons and for units of work covering a term or half term is also covered in the Non-Statutory Guidance. Examples are given for different activities and different age groups. This material is very useful as a starting point.

As far as assessment is concerned there is very little published material at the practical level needed by teachers. There are some references on page 103. We believe that effective assessment goes hand in hand with effective planning and good teaching. Good teachers are assessing all the time. You make judgements as you teach about how well an activity is going and how well children are coping with it and how much individuals are learning. The new factor for many teachers is recording children's progress in PE in a meaningful way. We believe that teachers can overcome this new problem if they plan in a more focused way to lead the children towards a small number of clear learning objectives. If the aim of your gymnastics lesson is for all the children to become more confident at taking their weight on their hands and you structure the lesson to enable that to happen, with plenty of relevant tasks and practices, it isn't too difficult to see whether the children achieve what you intend. You can note the few children who progress more slowly, and the few who may be ahead of the rest (and plan appropriate support or extension activities for them) and be fairly safe in the knowledge that most children have achieved your objective. In other words if you focus your planning enough your assessment will, to some extent, take care of itself. The way in which you record children's progress will depend on a number of factors but it is bound to be more helpful if a school has a consistent system which enables information about children's progress to be passed on from teacher to teacher. A number of schools have been using commercially produced record books for each pupil containing NC statements in table form with a space for a brief comment. In PE these are of limited usefulness because the End of Key Stage Descriptions are very general in nature. They are not designed to describe in detail what an individual can actually do. These descriptions need to be 'unpicked' so that teachers can identify a specific way in which a pupil has 'met' the description. It may be helpful for teachers to identify a list of core skills in each area of activity which most children would be expected to achieve at given ages. In the interim and final reports of the National Curriculum Working Party on PE there are examples given at ten levels of attainment and these can be a useful starting point.

The PE co-ordinator

Most schools have a 'postholder' or co-ordinator

for each subject including PE. Their experience and expertise varies from the well-trained specialist to someone with little training who has the role tagged on to a list of other responsibilities. In this situation it is hardly surprising if the co-ordination of PE across the school is less than dynamic. It is very important that a member of staff with some influence has the role of ensuring that PE figures appropriately in the life of a school. It can be ideal if this is the Head or another senior figure but expertise and enthusiasm have to be balanced against seniority. A young teacher with real flair can be very effective in supporting colleagues particularly because young teachers may have more recent experience of training in practical activities and new approaches to teaching. On the other hand there is no reason why an older person cannot be a really good teacher of PE and every reason why someone senior enough to influence important whole school decisions can be an excellent co-ordinator. In fact it is important that children see older people around them who clearly continue to value and enjoy physical activity. Understanding what children need to do and understanding the enormous importance of exercise are far more important than youth and the ability to demonstrate physical skills.

The size of a school obviously affects the number of incentive allowances available, so in the present funding system there cannot always be an appropriate allowance for co-ordinators of all subjects. Whatever the situation, it is crucial that PE is discussed by staff, features properly in whole school and individuals' planning and is given the status it deserves. PE (like music and art) is an important aspect of the work in a school. It is the job of the PE co-ordinator to ensure not only that the work is of a high standard but also that it is properly regarded by pupils and staff.

Who can teach what?

In most schools there will be individuals with particular weaknesses (for example in dance or gymnastics) and sometimes there will be people with real expertise or at least more confidence than other colleagues. It is important to have purposeful discussions about how particular expertise can be shared with other colleagues and how weaknesses can be supported. Clearly an effective co-ordinator will play a central role in such discussions. It may be that arrangements can be made for one teacher to run some INSET for colleagues on a professional training day where everyone could try out ideas for playground orienteering or some action ideas for dance or apparatus layouts for gymnastics etc. Another strategy is for a confident teacher to help a less confident colleague with planning. It may be possible for a Head to cover a class occasionally to release the PE co-ordinator (or anyone with particular expertise) to teach alongside a less confident colleague. This could consist of taking a class as a demonstration lesson or part of lesson, leading just one part of a lesson such as the warm-up, or simply being on hand while the class teacher teaches, to step in with advice or the occasional intervention as appropriate. This would then be followed up by a discussion so that the class teacher could gradually assume (or resume) a more self-reliant role. These are perhaps limited strategies within one school and they need to be supplemented. Collaboration with another school or schools in a cluster can result in the pooling of considerable expertise either for more specialised teaching or to raise the confidence of others. Above all it is crucial that delegated INSET funds are made available for training in PE as well as other important subjects.

Facilities

What facilities are there? What equipment and other resources are available? Some primary schools have grass playing fields as well as playgrounds and indoor facilities usually in the form of a multi-purpose hall. Inner city schools (often dating from the turn of the century) rarely have grass but usually have at least one hall indoors as well as hard surface playgrounds. Unless the school is unusually lacking in space, basic facilities should prove no obstacle to providing a good PE programme with a variety of activities and a healthy emphasis on exercise. It may be, however, that the range of equipment and small apparatus is less than ideal. Many primary and junior schools have large gymnastics apparatus (wall frames) of the Cave Southampton type which may date from the 1930s. This apparatus can be very useful but it is not uncommon for it to dominate people's thinking about teaching gymnastics with the result that an appropriate range of skills is not progressively learned and children spend too much time doing rather vague exploratory work involving climbing or swinging on ropes. More seriously it is quite common for the range of gymnastics mats, stools, benches and especially the small apparatus (bats, balls, quoits, beanbags etc.) to be very old. Though these resources may still be serviceable it is important that there are enough for all pupils in a session and that the equipment is appealing and suitable for the children to use. Many schools have a limited range of gym mats, for example, which are often old (and therefore limited in their cushioning effect) and heavy to handle. So one practical step towards a better curriculum is to make sure that a suitable proportion of a school's money is spent to upgrade PE resources to an acceptable standard. In some schools this may be unnecessary because sufficient funds have been devoted to PE. In others it will be long overdue.

Facilities For Gymnastics

- Activity mats light and small enough for infants to handle (say 1 x1.5m (3ft by 4ft)) as well as larger ones (at least enough for one between two in a class of 30).
- A range of stools, trestles movement tables, boxes and horses of various heights and sizes of top (again these should be light enough for small children to handle in twos or fours).
- A range of benches, planks, ladders and bars which can be used independently or hooked up to stools and trestles as well as fixed apparatus like Cave Southampton or infant foldaway.
- Several manufacturers now make attractive combination apparatus suitable for infants and juniors and up-to-date catalogues should be obtained.
- Landing mattresses or 'crash mats' can be useful especially for teaching more difficult agility skills but they are not necessary for normal class teaching.

Facilities For Games

- A selection of balls of different weights, sizes, shapes, colours, materials and textures and hardness – you need enough for one ball each for basic ball-skill lessons with young children. The range of products on the market is very wide and attractive so you need to choose examples which give a reasonable variety of characteristics of bounce. Above all, many balls should be available which are light and soft to catch and handle to encourage development of confidence.
- A selection of bats: short and fat; longer and thinner; one handed like table tennis bats; two handed like unihoc sticks and cricket bats. One important rule of thumb is: light, short-handled, wide-hitting surface bats are easy to use and produce likely success for young children. Long-handled, thin-hitting surface, heavy bats are difficult and more likely to result in failure. So a short tennis bat is suitable for most primary children, a rounders bat is not – at least not until hitting skills have been practised and mastered with easier implements.
- A selection of cones, skittles, marker discs, coloured bibs and bands as well as quoits, large shuttlecocks, bright coloured beanbags, hoops.
- A range of playground markings and targets on walls is useful as are rebound nets and frames of the kind used for the game 'Tchoukball'.

Facilities For Dance:

- A clean, warm work space without interruptions.
- A range of music on tape-cassette, a good twin-deck cassette player powerful enough to fill the space with sound, a variety of other sound stimuli (such as tambourines, castanettes, rattles, cymbals, xylophones etc.) including tuned musical instruments if someone is available to play.
- Visual and tactile stimuli including pictures, fabrics, wool and ribbons.

The Happy Heart Project has produced a cassette tape of lively music which is suitable for dance and for many kinds of active lessons.

It is essential that your working spaces are clean and safe. Many people will be familiar with the problems of multi-purpose halls which have to be vacated well before lunch time and then require cleaning if you don't want children doing their floor work amid the debris of stray peas and mashed potato. Similarly the playground really must be free of litter if possible so that there is no danger (from drinks cans and glass etc.) and the children can have a high-quality lesson. Schools also need to ensure that apparatus (like the Cave and foldaway) is serviced and safe. In these days of LMS and GMS this may be a matter for individual schools. LEA arrangements may no longer be there to rely on. But money must be set aside for these purposes just as they must for the hire of swimming pools and other essential facilities off-site even though the delegated budget does not earmark funds. Obviously these are a Head's responsibilities but Heads will be grateful to a co-ordinator who can alert them to these matters.

We provide a full list of recommmended apparatus and equipment in the Appendix (page 107).

Additional help

Is there additional adult help? In many schools primary helpers or classroom assistants support teaching in the classroom in a number of ways – for example hearing children read. If these helpers have useful experience or interest there seems to be no reason why they could not provide help with PE lessons too. Of course with limited primary helper or classroom assistant hours, Heads decide at which times their additional help will be used and it may be that supporting the teaching of reading or other important classroom work takes up all the support available. But it is worth investigating if the support can be extended to, or shared with, PE. Another possible angle to explore is the availability of parents to help during PE lessons. Some parents may have time and expertise to spare especially if they have been involved in appropriate activities. Of course any such help must be with the approval of the Head and teachers would need to talk through the principles of working with children and make sure that ground-rules are understood with any adults offering to help. Local sports development officers can help here by organising training which will enable interested people to become more skilled in activities and in working with children.

Extra-curricular activity

What extra-curricular activity is there? The range of activities available to children carries important messages about physical activity and its relevance to all pupils. Many teachers may feel, understandably, that they are fully committed and stretched by their classroom teaching and any administrative roles they have. But some teachers are still able to find the time and energy to organise clubs and teams. This being the case it is worth remembering that the final report of the National Curriculum Working Party on PE reminded us that especially for primary age children '. . . the game is not the thing, the child is'. So the ways in which extra-curricular clubs and teams are organised and the ways in which activities including competition are presented to children are all-important. We would urge very strongly that whatever activities are on offer should be open to all pupils of suitable age and that skill learning is at an appropriate pace and in suitable stages. Participation and enjoyment should be emphasised alongside success in competition. Extra-curricular activity is an ideal setting for help from parents if they have suitable interest and expertise. But even if adult helpers have no special expertise, training can be given in the principles of working with young children. The same applies to other adults in local clubs or sporting bodies. It is important that people realise they are dealing with children and not miniature adult sportsmen and women. Again local sports development officers can provide help in all sorts of ways.

Classroom work

What opportunities are there for work in the classroom about exercise? Appropriate classroom preparation and follow-up to practical PE lessons is essential. It is important, especially in the context of the likely development of more specialised teaching at the top of the primary school, that teaching about exercise is not confined to the practical sessions in the hall or playground. Teachers should ensure that children perceive what they do in PE as 'proper learning' by talking about it during preparation for the practical work and by reviewing it afterwards. Opportunities should also be taken to link classroom work whenever possible (certainly in science, language and mathematics, and probably in art and technology too) with appropriate aspects of exercise. It isn't always possible or reasonable to do this and contrived links are not helpful. But children are interested in their bodies and how they work, as well as in sports and games, so there are fairly regular opportunities to reinforce the idea that work about exercise has a place in the classroom. It is important here to remember that the HEA materials *My Body* and *Health for Life* provide many starting points for work on health issues including physical activity and exercise and will also offer valuable guidance in the way PE can contribute to the wider work in health education. *Health for Life* provides a planning framework for health education as well as teaching and learning materials for key areas. It is based on unique research in which children were asked to draw and write (with help if necessary) about what 'makes you healthy and keeps you healthy'. Many children focused on physical activity in their responses. The key to the materials and the project based at Southampton University (Promoting Health in Primary Schools) is the notion of starting from where children are. This is likely to be far more effective in enabling children to make positive decisions about their health-related behaviour than simply telling them what we think they ought to know.

Important messages

What messages are there in the school about sport and exercise?

Many schools have routines and ceremonies to do with physical activity such as awarding swimming or gymnastics badges in assembly and reading results of school matches. These can play a valuable part in establishing and reinforcing the importance of PE and sport in school, and in boosting the self-esteem of the individuals concerned. They are reinforcing the notion that children can achieve success through their own efforts. It is important that these and other rituals and routines like the selection of teams are handled well. They carry powerful messages for children which may affect their attitudes and feelings about themselves. Do we still pick teams (or allow children to choose teams) during lessons in a way which ensures that certain children will always be picked last? If too much emphasis is placed on rewarding the most successful and most able it may be that other children may begin to feel that it isn't worth trying too hard in physical activity. It is important that all children see their efforts acknowledged and praised when appropriate and that rewards and privileges for the most successful are kept in proportion. Children are well aware of differences in ability so these need not (and cannot) be disguised. The most able children should be encouraged as much as possible, without putting them under too much pressure relative to their stage of development and without encouraging inflated egos. But it is even more important to encourage children of all abilities to be involved in physical activity. With that in mind it is worth examining those rituals and routines to ensure that hidden messages are not saying to children that they are valued less than others.

What images of exercise are there around school?

Are there pictures on walls in prominent places reflecting a range of different activities and different groups of people? These could include posters, photographs and children's work on display and can be particularly valuable if children have a part in choosing them and deciding where they might go, as well as in producing their own work.

What publications are in the staffroom?

Is there a wide range of modern books, journals, magazines and resources on PE? There are now many information books, practical teaching guidelines and coaching guides available. Having a good range prominently displayed and accessible will not only be an immediate practical help to teachers but simply by being there will provide a message that PE and exercise are of central importance in the school. See the resources list of useful references (pages 103–5) to get some idea of what might help improve your school's teaching about health and fitness.

What magazines and other publications are available to pupils?

It is worth checking to see what the school library and class libraries contain in relation to exercise and sport. Is a wide range of activities reflected in the books and magazines you can find in the school for children to read? How old are the books? Is there a reasonable representation of the many groups in society and of both sexes and all ages? Is there a range of different kinds of publication – fiction and non-fiction books, magazines, newspapers? Can the range of publications appeal to all ages and the full range of reading ability? Are there any publications in languages other than English? Ensuring ready access to printed material and pictorial representation of appropriate images can create and help to sustain interest in health, and all forms of exercise for children.

What role models are there in school?

Children notice the way people look, the way they dress and the things they do. So it is important that, within reason, teachers and other adults provide role models which are as positive as possible. Children know perfectly well that people come in all shapes and sizes and have all kinds of interests which may or may not include sport.

Nevertheless there are some things which adults in schools can do about presenting appropriate images or role models. All teachers can make some effort to wear suitable clothes for practical PE lessons. Of course not everyone wants to (or should) demonstrate practical skills especially if they require particular agility, but everyone can put on comfortable clothing and shoes in which it is possible to move. At the very least all teachers should change into suitable shoes and ideally a tracksuit or jogging bottoms and a sweatshirt or some similar alternative. If there is no opportunity to change during the day why not simply come to school on PE days in your comfortable tracksuit and trainers? The message for children must be that this is something worth getting properly prepared for – and that we adults do it as well and we continue to enjoy it and value it too.

Is PE ever cancelled?

Are there times when you just don't feel like the effort of getting out all that apparatus? Do you ever get to the point when you say, 'Right! I've had enough if you can't be quiet we won't have PE'? Is PE ever pushed out by plays, parents evenings and other uses of the hall? Of course there are times when very important events are planned for the school hall, and they need to be taken into account so that alternative arrangements are made for PE. These things need careful thought and the priorities should be properly established and, if necessary, explained to the children. Do we tell them that we can't have our normal lesson because the hall is needed for something else but of course we can't miss the PE lesson so it will be in the infant hall (or the playground)?

Are there community links which relate to physical activity?

In many schools people are considering ways of using the premises to the full (and perhaps generating some income). So there may be opportunities of making links with community groups which have potential spin-offs for the schools in terms of promoting physical activity. There may be members of such groups using the premises who can make a contribution to teaching or coaching or INSET for staff if they have suitable expertise or experience. The activities of such groups can add other dimensions to the life of the school too. Perhaps there is a club playing short-mat bowls in the school hall: can that be made available to the children as well? The same might apply to a number of activities (archery, fencing, badminton) played indoors or outdoors which otherwise would not be accessible to children. The presence of other active people in schools can add to the number of images of sport and physical activity and positive role models which children see. Of course there are also lots of potential links outside the school. Children can be encouraged, ideally with their parents, to visit local leisure and recreation facilities and many schools will use local facilities(for example for swimming). The local health promotion unit will have resources to support teaching about exercise and health in general, as well as staff who can provide advice and support in all sorts of ways and perhaps teach in school as well.

This chapter has set out a number of areas for schools to consider. Some of them might be controversial. But if someone with vision and determination tackles one thing at a time and gradually wins over colleagues a great deal can be accomplished. We hope that you find material here to help you develop the climate in your school to be as supportive as possible to the promotion of healthy exercise for everyone.

5 Practical Lesson Ideas

This chapter contains three lessons for each of the six areas of activity in the National Curriculum for PE, together with five examples of complete units of work. They are intended to be seen as suggestions about ways in which you might teach about health and fitness in the context of exercise in different forms, and of health and physical education as a whole. We must emphasise that these lessons are intended to be seen as small components of a complete programme. The National Curriculum Non-Statutory Guidance in PE advises a modular approach to planning. This can provide progression and opportunities for a range of different themes within each area of activity. Each lesson in this chapter is one from a unit of six and is designed as an example forming part of the whole unit. Obviously you will need to add this to plan complete units of work in each area of activity. These lessons are starting points – suggestions about how you might think about and plan.

We have based these example lessons on the assumption that you will have about 35–40 minutes working time. Clearly the amount of time available for PE is a potential problem and many schools may be finding that they are unable to provide as much time as they would wish. The time taken to go to swimming lessons off-site is a particular concern for many schools. However, it is still important to bear in mind that children need to be physically active regularly (ideally at least three times a week for periods of at least 20 minutes). We recognise that three taught sessions a week may not always be practicable for all age groups, but we would hope that at least two substantial sessions will be timetabled. We would argue that this is essential for the sake of the children's health. Bearing in mind the need to organise apparatus and the time taken for changing clothes, we think that basing your planning around a 'working time' of 35–40 minutes is reasonable. This would include the setting out of equipment, warming up and cooling down, plus any pauses for explanation and discussion. In this way 20 minutes of actual exercise should be possible. Naturally teachers will want to train children to be as quick and efficient as possible at changing clothes. Of course this will develop gradually with infant children needing a lot of patient help in many cases, especially if shoe laces and ties are involved!

Setting up apparatus for gymnastics is a long-standing problem in some schools particulary where one hall has to be used for a range of purposes, including dinners. In such cases it is understandable that teachers decide, for example, to let older pupils set out apparatus for younger classes or develop arrangements where one class sets it out and the next puts it away. Such strategies for saving time are easy to understand, especially if teachers engage in joint planning so that the apparatus is designed specifically for the work in each lesson. However, if the apparatus is already out at the beginning of a lesson it can make appropriate warm-up and floor work difficult simply because the necessary floor space isn't available. The important point is that children should learn to lift, carry and place apparatus safely and sensibly as an integral part of the lesson. Arrangements where, for example, the schoolkeeper puts out the apparatus for the whole school on 'apparatus day' are just not acceptable. In these circumstances appropriate planning is almost impossible and because the apparatus is always the same there is an inevitable tendency for children simply to climb or play on the apparatus in ways which make real progression or development of skills very unlikely. Therefore an important part of teachers' planning must be to decide how equipment and apparatus will be placed ready for the beginning of the lesson and how the children will be organised to move it into position. With a little forethought and training of the children this need not take up very much time. It also helps if there is a good range of equipment available.

We have assumed in writing these materials that teachers will be planning for the full range of ability including very able children, physically and intellectually, and some who will have difficulty in learning or have disabilities which limit their participation or progress. Because of the very wide range of needs which may be found in any school we have chosen not to address the issue of special needs specifically in terms of providing a complete spectrum of planning ideas for all abilities. Instead we simply wish to emphasise that all children are entitled to experience fully all the benefits of challenging, enjoyable physical activity and exercise to help their physical development and growth, and to learn *about* health, physical activity, exercise and sport. We hope that we have provided enough help in the examples given for teachers to be able to modify the material, or see starting points, for all the children they teach.

Dance

KEY STAGE 1 (age 6–7)
ACTIVITY: DANCE BODY SHAPE

Aims of lesson

- To explore different body shapes, using balloons as a stimulus.
- To develop control and balance.
- To demonstrate lightness in movements.
- Encourage children to explore and use their own original/creative ideas in a short dance form.

National Curriculum – Relevance to End of Key Stage Descriptions and Programmes of Study

'Pupils plan and perform simple skills safely, and show control in linking actions together. They improve their performance through practising their skills working alone and with a partner. They talk about what they have done and are able to make simple judgements. They recognise and describe the changes that happen to their bodies during exercise.'

'Pupils should be taught ... to perform movements or patterns ... to explore moods and feelings ... to develop their responses to music through dances ... use rhythmic responses and contrasts of speed, shape, direction and level ... develop control, balance, co-ordination, poise, elevation, in their basic actions of travelling, jumping, turning, gesture and stillness.'

Health-related focus

National Curriculum Statement: 'pupils should be taught about the changes that occur to their bodies as they exercise ... to recognise the short-term effects of physical exercise on their body.'

The lesson activities will include work on stamina, strength, and suppleness; movements such as bending, twisting and stretching, with emphasis on balance and co-ordination.

Some movements will be slow and controlled requiring good body tension (tight muscles) – muscular strength. There will also be travelling in different body shapes, which will involve running, rolling, spinning, jumping – stamina. Most of the movements require bending, stretching and twisting which develop/require suppleness.

Preparation in the classroom

Teacher
You will need at least two inflated balloons. It would be a good idea to have a long/twisted balloon as well for the second part of the lesson. Pre-blow them before the lesson (do not knot!). It will be easier to blow them up during the lesson if you have already inflated them once before. Have a spare already blown up and tied.

Children
Ask the children why it is important to change before their dance lesson. Why are bare feet better for movement work than shoes? Ask them to remember how they feel during the lesson. What will we do first when we go into the hall or gym? (Warm-up.)

Warm-up

Activity in the working space	*Points to watch and questions to ask*
Light running in and out of spaces. Stopping and starting on command. Choose some general stretching from the suppleness bank (covering all major muscle groups)	Stress use of space – no touching Running quietly on the balls of the feet Safe and effective stretching (no bouncing, hold stretches). Good body tension.

Skills learning/development activities

Activity in the working space	*Points to watch and questions to ask*
(a) Blow up a balloon a puff at a time. Ask the children to be in a low curled shape on the floor, and to grow as you blow up the balloon. Stopping (freezing) each time you stop for a breath.	Emphasis on clear body shape. Tension and stillness when they hold the shape. Puff-out body (cheeks, stomach etc).
(b) Show how a blown-up balloon bounces high and lands softly and silently. Ask the children to practise jumping slowly on two feet – on the spot and around the area. Change directions and speeds.	Be aware of space Emphasise control on landings – 'give' with feet and knees. Land on balls of feet Use all directions (forwards, backwards, sideways, turning) Emphasise quality, lightness
(c) Demonstrate how a balloon drifts and floats smoothly, high and slow. Ask the children to be a wide balloon shape and to turn slowly, high/low spinning/rolling.	Keep tension in shape throughout movements Emphasise quality of lightness Emphasise bent legs, twisted trunks and heads Discuss different twists – ask children to show
(d) Practise rising and turning from a low curled position into a tall, twisted balloon shape and down again. Ask them to grow into their own twisted balloon shapes.	others their shapes/ideas Maintain body shapes and tension and keeping actions quiet. Extension of every body part (heads, fingers). Use whole body
(e) Extend into a long smooth balloon shape. Return to curled shape on floor, and extend to twisted shape. Return to floor.	Change of speed and directions Jumping, twirling, spinning actions Watch space and make sure there is no contact. Use of tension
(f) Show what happens when the air is released from a blown-up balloon. Ask the children to show how the balloon travels, fast, turning, jumping and then finally falling to the floor.	Space, changes directions Contrast in speeds

Dance

Ask children to start low in a curled position and grow into any balloon shape of their choice. Travel keeping the shape (smoothly and quietly). Clap when air is released from the balloons. Children travel and then come to rest on the floor. Practise and refine dance.	Use children to demonstrate good examples (e.g. whole body movements, maintaining body shape)

Cool-down

Activity in the working space	*Points to watch and questions to ask*
Choose any activity from the suppleness bank.	Emphasise safe and effective stretching. Calm children after an exciting dance.

Back in the classroom

Talk about the type of movements used in the lesson – did you feel like a balloon? Could others tell what sort of balloon you were? Did you become breathless during the lesson? How did this feel? Did you enjoy the lesson? Why? How did you feel when you were slowly stretching at the end of the lesson?

Evaluation

- Were all the children involved as much as possible?
- Did you manage to praise/encourage as many children as possible?
- Did you emphasise quality and control by using children to demonstrate?
- Did the children achieve lightness in the movements and clear body shapes?
- Do you think the children understood what was asked of them?
- Did they use whole body actions?
- Did they enjoy the lesson?
- What do they need to do next?

Progression and extension ideas

- Balloons continued – contrasting speeds, how a balloon bursts. Sudden fast movements, slow growing, sudden deflation
- Pairs and group work development
- Follow my leader
- Body shapes using mirror ideas. Distorted shapes. Copying each other's shapes
- Use of poetry, particularly shadows
- Ideas from objects, body shapes inspired by natural objects (logs, twigs, rocks, trees) and man-made (pencil, robots etc.)
- Moving from one shape to another – exploration of linking movements.

Cross-curricular work

English: Write a story showing an understanding of the rudiments of the story structure.
Task: 'I am a balloon and someone buys me and accidentally lets me go...' – encourage the children to structure the story with help as necessary around the flight, journey and ending.

Key Stage 2
Activity: Dance, body awareness

Aims of lesson

- To use imagination to create puppet characters
- To be aware of the types of movements required to portray the characters and sustain these qualities in movement
- To use different step patterns, changes of speed and directions
- To produce, practise and refine a short class dance which has a clear start, middle and end.

National Curriculum relevance to End of Key Stage Descriptions and Programmes of Study

> 'Pupils find solutions, sometimes responding imaginatively, to the various challenges that they encounter in the different areas of activity. They practise, improve and refine performance and repeat series of movements they have performed previously, with increasing control and accuracy. They work alone, in pairs and in groups, and as members of a team. They make simple judgements about their own and others' performance and use this information effectively to improve the accuracy, quality and variety of their own performance. They sustain energetic activity over appropriate periods of time, and demonstrate that they understand what is happening to their bodies during exercise.'
> 'Pupils should be taught . . . to compose and control their movements by varying shape, size, direction, level, speed, tension and continuity . . . to express feelings, moods and ideas . . . to respond to the music . . . to create simple characters and narratives in response to a range of stimuli through dance.'

Health-related focus

National Curriculum Statement: 'pupils should be taught to sustain energetic activity over appropriate periods of time in a range of physical activities . . .to understand the short-term effects of exercise on the body.'

The lesson does not contain any sustained stamina work. The children should therefore be given an extended running warm-up with a selection of general conditioning and suppling exercises. It is vital that you remind the children of the importance of warming up the body before exercise (raising pulse rate) and the need to maintain and improve flexibility/suppleness.

The lesson activities will involve travelling (stamina) and body tension (muscular endurance) but little work on suppleness.

Preparation in the classroom

Teacher

- Have the Pinocchio story ready to read to the children.
- If you can borrow a marionette to show the children this would be a useful teaching aid.
- Have you any simple percussion instruments for the children to use? If so, check they are available.
- Make sure you have your PE kit, or at least have changed into appropriate shoes for the lesson.

Children

- Tell the children the Pinocchio story. Make sure they are aware that Pinocchio is a string puppet or a marionette. Discuss other types of puppets.
- Demonstrate how a string puppet works – if you have one available.
- Explain that in the dance lesson today they will be pretending to be puppets and making up their own stories.
- Make sure all the children change appropriately.

Warm-up

Activity in the working space	*Points to watch and questions to ask*
(a) Running and skipping in and out of spaces.	Raise the heart rate. Ask the children how they feel when they stop. What changes do they notice?
(b) Choose a selection of general stretching exercises from the suppleness bank.	Emphasise safe and effective exercise.

Skills learning/development activities

Activity in the working space	*Points to watch and questions to ask*
(a) Lie the children on their backs in a space on the floor. Tell them they are marionettes and that you are the puppet master.	Lift single body parts stiffly. Flop back once 'string' has been released.
(b) Ask the puppets to stand, head leading.	Maintain a puppet shape (elbows raised, leg stiff, feet apart, back straight).
(c) Tell the children to imagine they have their own puppet master who is checking the strings. Jiggle elbows, lift knees etc.	Use all body parts: elbows, feet, shoulders, knees, backs, tummies. Facial expression.
(d) Pinocchio walks – slow jerky, knees high.	Sharp, jerky movements. Stiff and slow. Watch for space. Use particularly good examples to demonstrate to rest of class.
(e) Pinocchio runs.	Change of speed Watch spacing Emphasise keeping the puppet qualities.
(f) Pinocchio dances. Let the children create their own puppet dances. **NB.** Children may wish to work in pairs using percussion. One dances, one plays and change over.	Clear puppet shapes, Rhythmic, jerky actions.
(g) Ask the children to experiment being other puppets and toys from a toy box. • All become puppet soldiers – stiff walk and salute. • Rag dolls – floppy, swinging movements. • hard puppets – wide, stiff movements.	Let them use their imaginations. Encourage changes of directions and levels jumping, spinning, skipping etc.
(h) Choose any toy they wish from the toy box and make it come alive.	Stress that they must maintain the shapes and the qualities of the characters as they move.

Cool-down

Activity in the working space	*Points to watch and questions to ask*
Slowly stand and stretch out into a marionette puppet shape. Show tension.	Stress tension in puppet shape.
Slowly crumple and collapse onto the floor – totally relaxed.	Totally relaxed on the floor.
Puppet master checks all the puppets are relaxed and cuts the strings.	Go round to check all the puppets are relaxed.

Back in the classroom

Ask the children to describe the movements used in the dances. Was it easy to keep the puppet shapes and qualities? Does visual expression help? Did they enjoy the session? What could they do to improve the dance? (costume? own music? make-up?)

Evaluation

- Were all the children interested and involved?
- Did they manage to maintain the qualities required?
- Did they use their imaginations?
- Did you manage to praise and encourage as many children as possible?
- Did you use pupils to demonstrate good practice?
- What do they need to do next?

Progression and extension ideas

- Develop the dance idea further with costume, make-up and the children's own musical accompaniment.
- Children to work in pairs, one directing the puppet by being an imaginary puppet master.
- Develop set dance for the puppets (or soldiers) children will learn to keep together and in precise time – to practise and repeat a series of steps/actions.
- Small group dances. Each group make up their own "toybox" dance. Practise and show rest of the class in turn.
- Move on to other character dances – e.g. circuses (clowns, trapeze, tight rope walkers), at work (cook, waiters, bus drivers, typists etc).

Cross-curricular work

English – Speaking and Listening:
'Pupils are asked to relate real or imaginary events in a connected narrative which conveys meaning to a group of pupils, the teacher, or another known adult.'
Task: Describe what it feels like being a puppet kept in a play box. What is it like when you come out to play at night
What do you do? How does it feel?

Key Stage 2
Activity: Dance, general space – straight floor pathways

Aims of the lesson

- To explore straight pathways on the floor, using general space
- To vary types of steps, directions, levels and speeds in their movements
- To produce, practise and refine a short dance which has a clear start, middle and end.

National Curriculum – relevance to End of Key Stage Descriptions and Programmes of Study

'Pupils find solutions, sometimes responding imaginatively, to the various challenges that they encounter in the different areas of activity. They practise, improve and refine performance and repeat series of movements they have performed previously, with increasing control and accuracy. They work alone, in pairs and in groups, and as members of a team. They make simple judgements about their own and others' performance and use this information effectively to improve the accuracy, quality and variety on their own performance. They sustain energetic activity over appropriate periods of time, and demonstrate that they understand what is happening to their bodies during exercise.'
'Pupils should be taught . . . to compose and control their movements by varying shape, size, direction, level, speed, tension and continuity . . . to express feelings, moods and ideas . . . to respond to the music . . . to create simple characters and narratives in response to a range of stimuli through dance.'

Health-related focus

National Curriculum Statement: 'pupils should be taught to sustain energetic activity over appropriate periods of time in a range of physical activities . . .to understand the short-term effects of exercise on the body.'
The lesson activities will involve a thorough warm-up and body preparation section with emphasis on pulse raising followed by mobilising exercises which will promote suppleness. The theme of pathways provides the opportunity for travelling and promotes a degree of stamina work.

Preparation in the classroom

Teacher
- Check you have booked or have access to a cassette player (for warm-up particularly).
- Is the music at the correct starting point?
- You may use music for the step patterns. Children can work to an eight beat phrase for each line of the pattern. Any instrumental music with clear phrasing would be appropriate (e.g. 'Westaway' by Sky).

Children

Make sure all the children are appropriately dressed and all valuables have been collected and hair tied back.
Ask the children why this is important for all practical lessons.

Warm-up

Activity in the working space	*Points to watch and questions to ask*
Light running in and out of space stopping and starting on command Choose a selection of stretches from the suppleness bank.	Space, emphasis on using all the space and no touching Running quietly on the balls of the feet Use background music for stretches. Ensure they are performed slowly and correctly.

Skills learning/development activities

Activity in the working space	*Points to watch and questions to ask*
(a) Walking with good posture in straight lines, stop on command (marching)	Quality of movements. Head high, walking on balls of feet.
(b) As above vary size of steps (4 small, 4 large etc.)	
(c) As above changing directions along line (i.e. travel sidesteps, backwards and forwards but keeping in a straight line)	Long, deep walk, high on tiptoes etc. Use lines on floor if marked
(d) Walking, turn corner sharply on command continue.	Use drum or clap
(e) As above vary the type and direction of the steps.	Jumping, skipping, hopping
(f) Ask children to travel along 3 straight lines with sharp turns at corners) however they like on their feet. Ask individuals with original ideas to demonstrate to rest of the class.	Combinations with changes of direction Which movements are more easily performed fast or slow? e.g. Jumps – fast.
(g) Using the same pathway, get the children to repeat it using changes of speed (slow, fast, slow or fast, fast slow etc.)	Can be 'follow my leader' or simultaneous Suggest different starting places on the floor so could meet and part during the 'dance'
(h) *With partners:* Watch each others step pattern Choose one for both to learn practise together. Clear starting and finishing position.	Allow children to interpret as they wish Children watching should be quiet Give them things to look for (e.g. are there 3 clear straight pathways in the dances) Ask for comments at the end
(i) Half group to perform their step pattern so that the other half can watch. Change over.	Praise children – pick out original ideas or special mention.

Cool-down

Activity in the working space	*Points to watch and questions to ask*
Choose any activity from the suppleness bank.	Emphasis on safe and effective exercise Calming children before returning to the classroom.

Back in the classroom

Ask the children to draw out their pathways on paper, labelling the steps/speeds/directions used. Did they find it difficult thinking up ideas? Did it help watching others working? What made some sequences (step patterns) particularly good – aesthetic quality? tension? precise steps? variety?

Evaluation

- Were all the children involved as much as possible?
- Did you manage to praise/encourage all children?
- Did you use pupils to demonstrate?
- Did the children achieve quality in the movements?
- Do you think the children achieved the aims set for the lesson?
- What do they need to do next?

Progression and extension ideas

- Curved pathways on the floor. Combinations of curved and straight
- Writing their names or words on the floor using different step patterns
- Develop into a journey idea – straight and curved pathways over different terrains (e.g. hot sand – sharp movements, mid-slow and sustained). Build into a dance involving a journey. Effort/weight qualities.
- Move to more complex step patterns (5 basic jumps)
- Step patterns using different parts of the feet (body awareness)
- Work on jumping (landing, elevation, turning)
- Pathways in the air – using whole body actions with similar development to floor patterns.

Cross-curricular work

Art: Investigating and Making – applying the principles of colour mixing in making various kinds of images. Experiment with ways of representing shape, form and space.
Task: Trace pathways on a large piece of paper. Use different ways of producing texture on the pathways – different brush strokes, use of different materials to print textures (wood, cloth etc). Vary the colours so they contrast and mix/blend.

Athletics

Key Stage I (year 2)
Activity: Athletics, Games, Running Skills

Aims of the lesson (Focus)

- To practise and improve running skills.
- To develop an understanding of keeping within the limits of a marked (straight) channel.
- To build in an idea of "running your fastest", i.e. sprinting.

National Curriculum – relevance to End of Key Stage Descriptions and Programmes of Study

> 'Pupils plan and perform simple skills safely, and show control in linking actions together. They improve their performance through practising their skills, working alone and with a partner. They talk about what they and others have done, and are able to make simple judgements. They recognise and describe the changes that happen to their bodies during exercise.'
> 'Pupils should be taught ... elements of games play that include running ... to develop and practise a variety of ways ... of travelling ... different ways of performing the basic actions of travelling.'

Health-related focus

National Curriculum statement: 'pupils should be taught about the changes that occur to their bodies as they exercise ... to recognise the short-term effects of exercise on the body.'
The lesson includes stretching, bending, and balance movements with work stressing control and co-ordination into whole body actions. Work on strength and stamina aspects is also included. Part of the cooling down phase of the lesson can be used to engage the children in discussion as to how the activities have affected the way they feel following such exercise.

Preparation in the classroom

Teacher
Is the area to be used well marked or will there be a need for cones, discs or chalked lines to help organisation? Questions to set prior to the activities:
- How fast can *you* run?
- For how long? How far?
- Can you run in a straight line?

Children
Pose the questions:
- Is there anything we can do to help you run faster?
- What do you do with your head when you run?
- What do *you think* you should do with your head when you are running?
- How do you think you are going to 'feel' if you run at your fastest for a short period?
- What will we have to do to get ready for periods of fast running?

Warm-up

Activity in the working space	*Points to watch and questions to ask*
Choose an activity from the suppleness/ stamina bank.	Exercises focusing on good stretching and bending, preparing for activities that require short, sharp bursts of activity.

Skills learning/development activities

Activity in the working space	*Points to watch and questions to ask*
(a) Whole group behind a scratch starting-line – on command (whistle, voice 'Marks Set, Go', or clap of hands) run to marked finish, initially 10 metres away. 'how far can you run in 5/10 seconds?' Walk back to start and repeat	Head still to aid balance in running. Pumping arms? Run 'through' finish. Running straight? Concentration.
(b) Repeat, try to improve.	Highlight through demonstration.
(c) Practise arm 'pumping action', with head still as possible.	Vigorous arm action, head looking forward.
(d) Practise running / sprinting in pairs, one watching then change over	Develop through observation and giving individual help / support.
(e) Whole group final attempt over a longer distance (25 metres).	Emphasise 'running for fun' and 'running well'.

Skill performance/application

Activity in the working space	*Points to watch and questions to ask*
Pairs relay across 20 metres, pass to partner who 'takes' and returns to partners starting point. Repeat 3 or 4 times.	Pass over bean bag or quoit, or baton, to partner – encourage 'ready' position to receive.
Gather the whole group together – comment on the efforts of the group as a whole.	Teacher to observe individuals' running techniques – praise and encourage and support where necessary.

Cool-down

Choose an activity from the 'Cooling down' bank.

Back in the classroom

Comment on the effort and achievements:

- What needs improvement?
- What was the most difficult to do? The arm actions? Keeping the head still? Running in straight lines?
- How did we feel after each short, but sharp, run?
- What changes did you notice after running? Hot, quicker heart beat, breathing faster?
- What games involve running? What sports do you know that need the players to run fast?

Evaluation

- Did we achieve what we set out to do?
- Were the children fully involved?
- What difficulties did they have?
- Can we pinpoint general or specific problems?
- Did the individual work promote improvement?
- Was the partner work useful?
- What do we progress to in the next session?

Progression

- Shuttle runs to improve direction in running.
- More 'relay' type activities.
- Further consolidation of good running/sprinting technique.
- More 'static' practices for head position and arm action.
- Timings of individuals over varied distances.

Cross-curricular work

Mathematics – Handling data. Task: Make simple block graphs of distances each child ran in a given time (5–10 seconds).

Key Stage 2
Activity: Athletics, Long-jump Skills

Aims of the lesson (Focus)

- Developing the skills of jumping for distance.
- Improving the run-up link to jumping for distance.
- Progression in awareness of how jumps are marked, measured and recorded.

National Curriculum – relevance to End of Key Stage Descriptions and Programmes of Study

> 'Pupils find solutions, sometimes responding imaginatively, to the various challenges that they encounter in the different areas of activity. They practise, improve and refine performance, and repeat series of movements they have performed previously, with increasing control and accuracy. They work alone, in pairs and in groups, and as members of a team. They make simple judgements about their own and others' performance, and use this information effectively to improve the accuracy, quality and variety of their own performance. They sustain energetic activity over appropriate periods of time, and demonstrate that they understand what is happening to their bodies during exercise.'
> 'Pupils should be taught ... to develop and refine basic techniques in running, e.g. *over short distances, over longer distances, in relays*, throwing, e.g. *for accuracy/distance*, and jumping, e.g. *for height/distance*, using a variety of equipment ... to measure, compare and improve their own performance.'

Health-related focus

National Curriculum statement: 'pupils should be taught how to sustain energetic activity over appropriate periods of time in a range of physical activities ... the short-term effects of exercise on the body.'
The lesson activities include movements requiring stretching, bending, co-ordination in movement and balance, as well as elements of strength work. In the cool-down part of the lesson the children could be asked to reflect on the effects long-jump has on the body. Is a lot of strength required? Stamina? Suppleness?

Preparation in the classroom

Teacher
Revise previous work when jumping activities were involved.
What is a long-jump? How can we increase the distance we jump? How can individuals improve their own performance? How do we measure such jumps? Do we need any particular equipment to help with measuring?

Children
What will we need to do in preparation for jumping activities? What actions are needed when you 'long-jump'? Can you join these actions successfully?

Warm-up

Activity in the working space	*Points to watch and questions to ask*
Choose an activity from the suppleness bank	A balance between good stretching and some strength exercises will be needed here to prepare thoroughly for the movements to follow.

Skills learning/development activities

Activity in the working space	*Points to watch and questions to ask*
(a) Using a scratch line or take-off point practise two-footed jumps to two-footed landings.	Drive arms forward and upwards to assist flight, get weight forward for landing.
(b) Develop to one-footed take-off.	Jump off 'stronger' foot. Sprint to take-off point.
(c) Add a run-up – 5 metres, then 10.	
(d) Develop by stressing depth in the jump – jump for height *and* distance.	Drive up on take-off.
(e) Begin spotting/marking distance of jumps	Work in pairs, one jumping, one spotting – change over.
(f) Extend run-ups where needed.	Maximum speed needed at take-off point.
(g) Awareness of take-off point – the take-off board.	Build in concepts of fairness.
(h) Practise, improve, take a measurement.	By working with a partner (or in groups of 4) the measurements can be marked, and finally measured accurately.

This activity can be done indoors as well as on *dry* grass, and of course using available sandpits where they exist. These must be well dug, flat and free from litter. Make sure that mats cannot slip if using them for indoor lessons as jumping targets. Chalk markings for scratch lines will be needed indoors, and outdoors disc markers can be used to mark approximate length of jumps. If award schemes (e.g. 10-Step or 5-Star) are being used to support the work, record children's performances on the class record sheets, or the computer data base (the children could do this too!).

Closing activity

Activity in the working space	*Points to watch and questions to ask*
Contrasting activity – whole group on stamina run for 3 minutes, to be done at individual's steady speed.	Emphasise the need to concentrate on basic running technique – head still, relaxed arms working on a good controlled style.

Cool-down

Choose an activity from the cooling down bank.

Back in the classroom

- Review individuals/whole groups efforts.
- Areas needing further practice identified.
- Which particular skill within the long-jump is in need of further work? Jumping for height? Use of arms? The run-up?
- How did we measure? What do we need to do to measure accurately? What do we measure with?

Evaluation

- Were the aims of the lesson fulfilled?
- Did the children work well individually? In pairs? Groups?
- Was your organisation good/
- Was there praise? Encouragement? Interaction?

- What was your overview of the general standard achieved?
- How should the work develop next?

Progression and extension ideas

- Jumping skills – More individual work, in open space, from take-off boards/lines/markings. Further emphasis on springing action required, and correct use of the arms to assist flight.
- Run-up – More specific focus on good sprinting technique and achieving a maximum speed at the take-off point.
- Linking the two skills – Good fast approach to top speed, spring for height and long-distance jumping.

Cross-curricular

Art – Investigating and Making – experiment with pattern and texture in designing and making images and artefacts. Task: Make replica athletics medals; make an Olympic torch.

Art – Knowledge and Understanding – understand and use subject specific terms such as landscape, still-life and mural. Task: Design and make a class mural depicting Olympic events and athletes performing particular events (at the track, swimming pool, gymnasium, etc.).

Key Stage 2
Activity: Athletics, Throwing Skills

Aims of the lesson (Focus)

- To develop an overarm throwing action
- To experience an 'explosive' action demanding physical competence in a 'natural' activity – i.e. throwing
- To learn about what is measured when throwing in athletics – i.e. distance
- To learn correct throwing techniques.

National Curriculum – relevance to End of Key Stage Descriptions and Programmes of Study

> 'Pupils find solutions, sometimes responding imaginatively, to the various challenges that they encounter in the different areas of activity. They practise, improve and refine performance, and repeat series of movements they have performed previously, with increasing control and accuracy. They work safely alone, in pairs and in groups, and as members of a team. They make simple judgements about their own and others' performance, and use this information effectively to improve the accuracy, quality and variety of their own performance. They sustain energetic activity over appropriate periods of time, and demonstrate that they understand what is happening to their bodies during exercise.'
> 'Pupils should be taught ... to develop and refine basic techniques in running, *e.g. over short distances, over longer distances, in relays*, throwing, *e.g. for accuracy/distance*, and jumping, *e.g. for height/ distance*, using a variety of equipment ... to measure, compare and improve their own performance.'

Health-related focus

National Curriculum statement ... 'pupils should be taught how to sustain energetic activity over appropriate periods of time in a range of physical activities ... the short-term effects of exercise on the body'.
This lesson includes and requires actions that combine a full range of movement (particularly in the shoulder joints) with application of strength and the development of increased co-ordination. These should be balanced by some sustained activity in the warm-up to develop stamina (as well as preparing the muscles for stretching) and thorough stretching of all major muscle groups.

Preparation in the classroom

Teacher
Revise previous throwing activities (with bean bags, quoits, various balls of different shapes and sizes):
- What have we thrown? How have we thrown (what actions have we used)?
- What objects travel furthest? Why? (Heavy, light, soft, hard, etc.)
- What equipment do we need to practise and learn about throwing? – i.e. balls of different kinds, markers (discs, cones, etc. If not available old washing-up bottles painted in bright colours and filled with sand for weight make excellent individual distance markers).
- What do we need to think about to make sure everyone is safe in the teaching/working area?

Children
- What kind of action is a throw? Are there different types? Pushing, pulling, slinging, etc. – quick, whipping action, one handed, two handed?
- Do I throw better underarm or overarm, with big objects or small, heavy or light?

Warm-up

Activity in the working space
Choose activities from the stamina and the suppleness bank.

Points to watch and questions to ask
Make sure the children are all involved in 4–7 minutes of light but continuous exercises which include a series of mobilising and stretching exercises especially for the shoulders, back and arms.

Skills learning/development activities

Activity in the working space

(a) Organise the children facing the same direction – establish a 'throwing line'.
(b) Ask them to practise throwing in two or three different ways. Use a number of demonstrations. Ask the children to try throwing overarm into the ground just ahead of themselves.
(c) Ask them to use the same action (bent elbow, wristy action) throwing to a partner across a large space (approx. 20 metres).
(d) Individually throw for distance from behind the safety/throwing line.
(e) Get the children to mark their partner's throw with markers available. (This could initially be done by pacing out or using pigeon steps.) Measure with tape the best of three throws. Build in 'beat your best' idea.

Points to watch and questions to ask
Make sure the children use a variety of small balls according to size, their ability, etc. Get the children to grip the ball lightly in their fingers – *not* in the palm.
Safety: Make sure everyone stays behind the throwing line until you tell them to collect the balls.

Ensure adequate spacing between individuals on each side of the throwing lines.
Work on throwing from a side-on position – opposite foot forward from throwing arm. Aim to release with the arm fully extended and at an angle of 30–40° to the ground.
Add a short run-up once the children begin to show increased accuracy and control.
Get the children to use the momentum of the run-up fully.

With safety considerations to the fore light, soft implements should be used initially; once there is a discernible appreciation of the need for control and accuracy on display, heavier equipment (which will go further) can be used.

Back in the classroom

Let the children tell you their impressions of the lesson. Ask them to say if they think they have improved their throwing actions and discuss why. Ask which parts of the lesson were the most difficult. Ask which aspects need to be improved and if there are ways of practising the throwing action in other activities the class does. Talk about the measuring. Talk about ways in which the measuring could be recorded.

Evaluation

- Were all the aims of the lesson fulfilled?
- How did the children respond to the tasks?
- Were they appreciative of the need for safety factors within the lessons activities?
- Did the children's throwing improve?
- Was your organisation effective? Individuals/pairs/groups?
- What do the children need to do next? Strong throwers, less strong, etc.

Progression and extension ideas

- Practise with different balls – e.g. cricket, rounders balls.
- Encourage all the children to add a run-up.
- Practise throwing at visible targets/areas to improve accuracy.
- Work in pairs across wide and long areas for further skill development.
- Work on different techniques – two-handed throw overhead (soccer style), straight arm sling (discus style), etc.

Cross-curricular work

- Maths – measuring and recording skills (data handling).
- English – speaking and listening, writing for a variety of purposes; use of new words to describe throwing actions.
- Science – using muscles, forces, projectiles etc.
- History/Geography – Ancient Greeks, Olympics (discus, javelin, shot, hammer throwing events).
- Religious Education – David and Goliath.

Key Stage 1
Activity: Games, Bat and Ball Skills

Aims of the lesson (Focus)

- To develop hand/eye co-ordination.
- To experience using different types and sizes of balls in different situations.
- To involve the children in running, dodging, stretching and bending movements.

National Curriculum – relevance to End of Key Stage Descriptions and Programmes of Study

> 'Pupils plan and perform simple skills safely, and show control in linking actions together. They improve their performance through practising their skills, working alone and with a partner. They talk about what they and others have done, and are able to make simple judgements. They recognise and describe the changes that happen to their bodies during exercise.'
> 'Pupils should be taught ... simple competitive games, including how to play them as individuals and, when ready, in pairs and in small groups ... to develop and practise a variety of ways of sending (including throwing, striking, rolling and bouncing), receiving and travelling with a ball and other similar games equipment ... elements of games play that include running, chasing, dodging,avoiding, and awareness of space and other players.'

Health-related focus

National Curriculum statement: 'pupils should be taught about the changes that occur to their bodies as they exercise ... to recognise the short-term effects of exercise on the body.'
The lesson activities include movements such as stretching, bending, co-ordination and balance work. Stamina aspects are dealt with through rolling and running actions, individually and in a game situation. Suppleness is included within the need to stretch and bend as in reaching for the ball.
The cooling down period will help to focus on knowledge of health matters, with awareness raised of the importance of good posture. During this period pupils can be reminded of questions to take back to the classroom for follow-up work.

Preparation in the classroom

Teacher
Is there easy and immediate access to the equipment required? If not, time organising and getting out the equipment will need to be given to address such an important aspect of planning and teaching.

Is the equipment appropriate? Do you need a variety of equipment to suit the differing learning needs of the children? Are you aware of the floor markings in the workspace? Will you need to utilise marker discs or playground chalk to assist with this? Are there wall rebound spaces to practise the skills in the lesson?

Children
Set the mood and tone of the session by posing the following:
- What will we do first when we get to the workspace? (Warm-up!)
- 'When we are working today I'd like you to think about what's happening to your body' (Heart rate raised, puffing, getting hot, stiff, aching.)
- 'When we come back to the classroom we will talk about this, so make sure you are thinking (as well as doing!) throughout the lesson.'
- 'Why do you think we should change if we are going to run about?' (Health and hygiene issues.)

Warm-up

Activity in the working space	*Points to watch and questions to ask*
Choose activities from the stamina bank.	A skills-based lesson requires a vigorous warm-up which will get the children puffing and warmed up properly for what is to follow.

Skills learning/development activities

Activity in the working space	*Points to watch and questions to ask*
(a) Each pupil takes a ball, places it on the floor, and moves the ball side-to-side using palms of hands – develop adding travel. Continue, and travel in different directions avoiding others – inject a change of pace when possible.	Eyes following the ball. Keep regular contact with the ball. Encourage control and accuracy.
(b) Into pairs – 'pat the ball between you' (c) Introduce a 'gate' (approx. 1metre wide) and aim each strike through to partner.	Head in line – position side-on each strike made – keep the ball on the floor Build a mini-rally

Skill performance/application

Activity in the working space	*Points to watch and questions to ask*
How many strikes consecutively can you and your partner make?	Count the rally – beat your best as a pair Start the count again when the ball leaves the floor, or control is lost.

Introduce padder bats, short tennis rackets, other shaped bats that will give high levels of success to the children – repeat individual and partner practices, and apply the skills in the game situation.

Cooling down

Choose an activity from the cooling down bank – have an emphasis on safe and effective stretching, and a calming input in readiness for a controlled return to the classroom.

Back in the classroom

Engage the children in discussion about what they have been doing – what skills they have practised, the mini-game they had played with partners, what they would like to do next session to help them improve, how they felt at the end of the session: tired? excited? wanting more of the same!

Evaluation

- Were all the children involved as much as possible?
- Was there a high level of activity within the session?
- Was there a good balance of skills practised? Footwork skills as well as hand/eye co-ordination?
- Did you as the teacher manage to praise/encourage as many of the children as possible?
- Did the children learn 'new' skills? How do you know? What is the evidence?
- What do they need to do next?

Progression and extension ideas

More individual work with a variety of bats, extending the work to use rebound surfaces. Introduce a 'one-bounce before we hit' practice against the rebound surface before we further progress the partner work.
Mini-court set-ups – 2 x 1 metres, and the possibility of low 'nets' (using canes or skipping-ropes and skittles). Developing the idea of continued co-operative play, but introducing an element of competitiveness too.

Cross-curricular work

Mathematics and language:
Counting the number of passes made, measuring the size of the court or height of the net.
Using words like: high and low, hard and soft, glide, strong, forwards, backwards, sideways.

Key Stage 2
Activity: Games, Hockey skills

Aims of the lesson (Focus)

- To develop co-ordination skills.
- To learn to propel, field and control balls with a hockey stick.
- To introduce the basic skills of hockey and how to apply them into a basic game.

National Curriculum – relevance to End of Key Stage Descriptions and Programmes of Study

> 'Pupils find solutions, sometimes responding imaginatively, to the various challenges that they encounter in the different areas of activity. They practise, improve and refine performance, and repeat series of movements they have performed previously, with increasing control and accuracy. They work safely alone, in pairs and in groups, and as members of a team. They make simple judgements about their own and others' performance, and use this information effectively to improve the accuracy, quality and variety of their own performance. They sustain energetic activity over appropriate periods of time, and demonstrate that they understand what is happening to their bodies during exercise'.
> 'Pupils should be taught ... to understand and play small-sided games and simplified versions of recognised competitive team and individual games, covering the following types – invasion, e.g. mini-soccer, netball, striking/fielding, e.g. rounders, small-sided cricket, net/wall, e.g. short tennis ... common skills and principles, including attack and defence, in invasion, striking/fielding, net/wall and target games ... to improve the skills of sending, receiving, striking and travelling with a ball in the above games'.

Health-related focus

National Curriculum statement: 'pupils should be taught how to sustain energetic activity over appropriate periods of time in a range of physical activities ... the short-term effects of exercise on the body'.

The lesson will include stretching, running, turning and twisting movements. The skill learning section of the session will involve vigorous exercise and will work on increasing levels of stamina.

Preparation in the classroom

Teacher

Is there easy and immediate access to the equipment required? If not, time organising and getting out the equipment will need to be given to address such an important aspect of planning, teaching and learning.

Is the equipment appropriate? A range of different sized hockey sticks and/or Unihoc sticks with appropriate balls (and pucks if available) will be needed for this session. Are you aware of the floor markings in the workspace? You will need to utilise marker discs or playground chalk to assist with this.

Children

Establish the key skills to be worked on in the session and re-affirm:
- The importance of a good 'warm-up' at the start of the session.
- Safety aspects – no sticks to be raised above hip level.
- Good use of the space and marked areas for practice.
- Ensure the children are fully aware of what is expected of them, particularly with regard to co-operative work.
- Are they motivated/enthused? Ensure they are by detailing both expectations and the 'fun' aspect from useful and purposeful activity.

Warm-up	
Activity in the working space Pick an activity from the warm-up bank – ensure it includes practice with small balls	*Points to watch and questions to ask* Monitor the level of group activity – ensure all are involved.

Skill learning/development activities	
Activity in the working space • Individually with stick and ball walk around keeping close control, and avoiding collision with others. Those using Unihoc sticks use both sides of the stick; those using hockey sticks use only the blade. • Develop to jogging practising same skills. • In pairs hit and stop the ball; move onto a 'push' action • In squared grid dribble ball from corner to corner, then pass across to partner; aim to keep control and pass in front of partner to help their receiving.	*Points to watch and questions to ask* Head over the ball; left hand at top of stick; right hand two-thirds of the way down the shaft of the stick; keep the ball 'outside' of stance and movement; keep ball close to the head of the stick. Side-on position; head in line with the ball; bend knees, firm grip, eye on the ball; 'give' when receiving. As above and also observe how the children run with the stick and are partners in a ready position to receive

Skill performance/application	
Activity in the working space In grids play 2 *v* 1 with adaptations according to ability: • defender in middle is 'passive' • defender walks to try and intercept • defender restricted to a hoop or centrally marked grid • develop to allow defender increasingly more scope to intercept as skill levels improve • rotate roles at regular intervals • If 2 *v* 1 is too difficult use 3 *v* 1 to ensure success	*Points to watch and questions to ask* Are the 'attackers' moving into space to receive? Are they developing disguise/feint/dummy plays to succeed in passing the ball? Are they looking at the ball and aware of the position of their partner and the defender? Are the children aware of the link between the skill learning and a game situation? Are they developing an understanding of attack and defence? Are team skills emerging as a result of a 2 *v* 1 situation?

Cool-down

Choose an activity from the cooling down bank once all the equipment is put away – calm and effective stretching (review, as you go, the key teaching points from the session, good play, and highlight what might need to be practised next to improve the quality of the game).

Back in the classroom

Engage the children in discussion about what they thought of the session. Do they have ideas about what extra skills they need to practise in order to improve their own performance level? What 'new' games could they play – how about 3 *v* 1 or 3 *v* 2 or 2 *v* 2, etc. What extras could be added to move towards a fuller and more 'real' game?

Evaluation

- Were all the children active and participating?
- Did individuals understand what was required and improve their techniques after practice?
- Were the children appropriately challenged to their individual ability level?
- Did they work 'physically' hard, raise their breathing rate, 'puff' at certain points in the session?
- Was the lesson fun?
- Did you as the teacher manage to praise/ encourage as many of the children as possible?
- What do the children need to do next?

Progression and extension ideas

Review the session through discussion afterwards. Repeat the session and develop the game part through 2 *v* 2, 3 *v* 3, etc., and introduce targets for the push pass fielding skills. Onto small-sided games, with basic rules and with mini-goals – gradually increase the complexity of the game.

Cross-curricular work

Science – friction and forces.
History – terminology and the use of 'Invasion' principles.

Key Stage 2
Activity: Games, Ball Handling and Invasion Games

Aims of the lesson (Focus)

- To develop skills of throwing, catching and travelling.
- To introduce the concept of space, momentum and team work.
- To involve children in running, dodging, passing and receiving a ball.

National Curriculum – relevance to End of Key Stage Descriptions and Programmes of Study

> 'Pupils find solutions, sometimes responding imaginatively, to the various challenges that they encounter in the different areas of activity. They practise, improve and refine performance, and repeat series of movements they have performed previously, with increasing control and accuracy. They work safely alone, in pairs and in groups, and as members of a team. They make simple judgements about their own and others' performance, and use this information effectively to improve the accuracy, quality and variety of their own performance. They sustain energetic activity over appropriate periods of time, and demonstrate that they understand what is happening to their bodies during exercise.'
> 'Pupils should be taught ... to understand and play small-sided games and simplified versions of recognised competitive team and individual games, covering the following types – invasion, eg mini-soccer, netball, striking/fielding, e.g. rounders, small-sided cricket, net/wall, e.g. short tennis ... common skills and principles, including attack and defence, in invasion, striking/fielding, net/wall and target games ... to improve the skills of sending, receiving, striking and travelling with a ball in the above games.'

Health-related focus

National Curriculum statement: 'pupils should be taught how to sustain energetic activity over appropriate periods of time in a range of physical activities ... the short-term effects of exercise on the body'.

The lesson activities encourage the pupils to move, run, twist, jump, dodge. Both stamina and suppleness aspects are part of this, as well as balance, co-ordination and the ability to play a game with others.

Preparation in the classroom

Teacher
Is there easy and immediate access to the equipment required? If not, time organising and getting out the equipment will need to be given to address such an important aspect of planning and teaching.

Is the equipment appropriate? Do you need a variety of equipment to suit the differing learning needs of the children? Are you aware of the floor markings in the workspace? Will you need to use marker discs or playground chalk to assist with this issue?

Children
Set the mood and tone of the session by posing the following:
- What will we do first when we get to the workspace? (Warm-up!)
- When we are working today I'd like you to think about what's happening to your body. (Heart rate raised, puffing, getting hot, stiff, aching.)
- When we come back to the classroom we will talk about this, so make sure you are thinking (as well as doing!) throughout the lesson.
- Ensure the children are fully aware of what is expected of them.
- Are they motivated/enthused? Ensure they are by detailing both expectations and the 'fun' aspect from useful and purposeful activity.

Warm-up

Activity in the working space	*Points to watch and questions to ask*
Choose an activity from the stamina bank (preferably one involving the use of balls).	Gradual increase in the pace of the activity. Use the warm-up to develop and practise personal skills.

Skills learning/development activities

Activity in the working space	*Points to watch and questions to ask*
(a) In pairs throwing and catching skills	Which different ways can you transfer the ball(s) to your partner? Can you spin it? Can you throw it higher? Can you do a chest pass, a bounce pass, a javelin pass, a lob pass? Passer – follow through, think about trajectory, where is the ideal target? Receiver – hands towards the ball, 'give' when receiving, fingers spread. How will you pass it back once you have possession?
(b) In pairs move freely in space and pass to your partner – STOP when you receive but otherwise keep moving	Pass in front of your partner – ensure that others working are not blocking the path of your pass.
(c) How many passes can each pair make without losing control? (d) In 3's, 4's – same practices	Judge the standard and increase the pace. Is this a successful exercise when speeded up? If not slow it down find the correct levels for the range of abilities.

Skill performance/application

Groups of 8 for 4 *v* 4. Development of skills to team game with conditions: • each team member must touch the ball before a score can be made • 'pivoting' skills are allowed when in possession • restricted zone around target areas • no physical contact allowed; once in possession allow 5 seconds to release ball	Skittle Ball, where teams must pass and move when not in possession in order to score (by knocking over a target skittle(s) – watch footwork. Alert to need to play defence, attack, etc. Encourage a wide variety of different types of passes as practised earlier. 'Freeze' play to pinpoint need to find space

Cool-down

Choose an activity from the cooling down bank once all the equipment is put away – calm and effective stretching (review, as you go, the key teaching points from the session, good play, and highlight what might need to be practised next to improve the quality of the game).

Back in the classroom

Engage the children in discussion about what they thought of the session. Do they have ideas about what extra skills they need to practise in order to improve their own performance level? What 'new' rules or conditions would they like to put into the game?

Evaluation

- Were all the children involved as much as possible?
- Was there a high level of activity within the session?
- Was there a good balance of skills practised? Footwork skills as well as hand/eye co-ordination used in the passing and receiving?
- Was the level of teamwork good?
- Was the lesson fun?
- Did you as the teacher manage to praise/encourage as many of the children as possible?
- Did the children learn 'new' skills? How do you know? What is the evidence?
- What do they need to do next?

Progression and extension ideas

Games including travelling with the ball – different targets, e.g. bench goals, target lines with a team-mate behind as a target to get the ball to, mini-goals, larger restricted zones, etc.
Vary rules – one-handed passes only, weaker hand pass only, restricted areas for certain players (defenders allowed only to half-way), etc. Extend/limit space of playing area to suit larger game, or confined to maximise finding space initiative.

Cross-curricular work

Making Games – write up the skills and rules and draw a diagram of the court of play. Detail the scoring system – points or goals?

Gymnastics

Key Stage 1
Activity: Gymnastics, 'Quiet Bodies'

Aims of the lesson (Focus)

- To establish an idea of what 'quiet bodies' are and how to achieve 'quietness'.
- To encourage originality and sensitivity in and through movement activities.
- To establish an understanding of action words.

National Curriculum – relevance to End of Key Stage Descriptions and Programmes of Study

'Pupils plan and perform simple skills safely, and show control in linking actions together. They improve their performance through practising their skills, working alone and with a partner. They talk about what they and others have done, and are able to make simple judgements. They recognise and describe the changes that happen to their bodies during exercise.'
'Pupils should be taught ... different ways of performing the basic actions of travelling using hands and feet, turning, rolling, jumping, balancing, swinging and climbing, both on the floor and using apparatus ... to link a series of actions both on the floor and using apparatus, and how to repeat them.'

Health-related focus

National Curriculum statement: 'pupils should be taught about the changes that occur to their bodies as they exercise ... to recognise the short-term effects of exercise on the body.'
The lesson activities include work on suppleness and strength. Maintaining activity over short time spans will offer opportunities for a degree of stamina work.

Preparation in the classroom

Teacher
Discuss the content of the planned lesson; recap past week's work, and recall general standards achieved to date. Set the opening 'travelling task' so that the children can move straight into their work once they enter the work space. Think about the potential for partner work, and ways of organising it.

Children
Respond to the teacher's promptings by talking about their actions of previous weeks. They need to be encouraged to think about their own personal response to the movements expected of them once they enter the workspace.

Warm-up

Activity in the working space	*Points to watch and questions to ask*
Travel near to the floor: in different ways – 'See how quietly you can move': • in different directions; • at different speeds/on different body parts.	Comment on what you see. Pick out general points as well as qualitative statements. Note spatial awareness.

Skills learning/development activities	
Activity in the working space	*Points to watch and questions to ask*
(a) Find a way of rolling – repeat.	Look for the shape here.
(b) Find a way to jump – repeat.	Emphasise bent knees on take-off and likewise for cushioning landings.
(c) Work on hands and feet. Work towards taking weight on hands (even momentarily). Repeating this activity will strengthen arms and shoulders.	Emphasise feet coming down quietly – 'placing' them back on the floor Emphasise hands spaced shoulder width apart and fingers pointing forward for safety.

Apparatus work	
Activity in the working space	*Points to watch and questions to ask*
Establish groups of 4. Erect apparatus, specifying area and the particular pieces to work on (allow some independent thought and decision-making here) Tasks: Work on, around, across, over, under, up, down using the basic actions of travelling i.e. jumping, rolling, balancing and taking weight on different body parts.	Safety aspects – quiet and controlled erection of apparatus. Check the fixings/linkages, landing areas and potential hazards. Emphasise: 1. Quiet bodies. 2. Awareness of others as you work. Use relevant demonstrations to highlight and consolidate the work.

Closing activity	
Activity in the working space	*Points to watch and questions to ask*
'Practise your favourite jump again. Check your knees bend, and that your hips go down on landing'.	Allow half the group to demonstrate to the other half; rotate. Invite comment.

Cool-down

Choose an activity from the suppleness bank.

Back in the classroom

- Discuss what the children have been doing.
- How it might develop in the next lesson.
- Highlight specific actions performed (and responses to them) covered in the lesson.
- Lead into the possibilities, activities and challenges to be set in the next lesson.

Evaluation

- Were the aims of the lesson fulfilled?
- What level of understanding of 'action words' was achieved?
- Did all the children respond to the tasks set?
- How well were the tasks answered?
- Did the class work safely and with awareness of others?
- Did you respond positively, praise and encourage regularly throughout the lesson?
- What needs further consolidation in the next session?

Progression and extension ideas

- Develop understanding of the difference between movements, and the variety possible.
- Other ways of rolling, jumping, taking weight on different body parts.
- Add more apparatus; change group composition; alter apparatus set-up.
- Different ways of moving on the apparatus as a result of experiencing a full range of movement possibilities.
- Individualise improvements, e.g. John's landings.

Cross-curricular work

Science – Life and Living Processes.
Topic work on 'the way living things move'.

Key Stage 2
Activity: Gymnastics, 'Travelling'

Aims of the lesson (Focus)

- To identify and build on the general level of movement ability in the group.
- To set realistic targets that match individual abilities.
- To develop an understanding of the theme of 'Travelling'.

National Curriculum – relevance to End of Key Stage Descriptions and Programmes of Study

> 'Pupils find solutions, sometimes responding imaginatively, to the various challenges that they encounter in the different areas of activity. They practise, improve and refine performance, and repeat series of movements they have performed previously, with increasing control and accuracy. They work alone, in pairs and in groups, and as members of a team. They make simple judgements about their own and other's performance, and use this information effectively to improve the accuracy, quality and variety of their own performance. They sustain energetic activity over appropriate periods of time, and demonstrate that they understand what is happening to their bodies during exercise.'
> 'Pupils should be taught ... different means of turning, rolling, swinging, jumping, climbing, balancing and travelling on hands and feet, and how to adapt, practise and refine these actions, both on the floor and using apparatus ... to emphasise changes of shape, speed and direction through gymnastic actions ... to practise, refine and repeat a longer series of actions, making increasingly complex movement sequences, both on the floor and using apparatus'.

Health-related focus

National Curriculum statement: 'pupils should be taught how to sustain energetic activity over appropriate periods of time in a range of physical activities ... the short-term effects of exercise on the body'.

The lesson activities emphasise body control through movement requiring suppleness, strength and a degree of stamina work.

Preparation in the classroom

Teacher
Review work covered to date; general reaffirmation of key movement skills involved. What is 'travelling'?: give a general backcloth to understanding for movement purposes. Set the initial movement task for when the group enter the workspace.

Children
What do the children understand about 'travelling'? How does their body 'move' and in how many different ways? How do changes of speed, direction and working at different levels affect the way we move?

Warm-up	
Activity in the working space	*Points to watch and questions to ask*
Walk anywhere – be aware of others. Think about the different directions you can move in.	Spatial awareness – of oneself and as one of a group.
Run on the spot, run anywhere – move lightly and with control.	Skilfulness, lightness, awareness of space and of others.
Bouncing actions on the spot – bounce anywhere.	Feet slightly apart – emphasise 'give' on landing, lower hips to help control/cushion landing.

Skills learning/ development activities	
Floorwork activities	
Activity in the working space	*Points to watch and questions to ask*
Introduce ideas of different levels and different speeds.	Encourage and explain how to make changes in levels and speed.
(a) Travel on hands/feet/ and other body parts.	Watch what the children do – comment on what you see.
(b) Travel by jumping/taking weight on hands. Make up various combinations of these actions.	Pick out examples for everyone to watch.
(c) Join 3 of these different actions.	Encourage the children as individuals – praise and highlight where appropriate.
Apparatus work	
Organise 6 groups and 6 areas to locate apparatus in. In setting-up stress the importance of constructing a layout with 'travelling' tasks in mind.	Safety aspects, sufficient numbers of children to each piece of apparatus; quiet and controlled setting-up. Emphasise awareness of others as they move individual pieces to areas allocated. Children to sit down next to their apparatus (*not on it*) once it is fully assembled. Teacher checks linkages and fastenings.
Tasks:	
(a) Where can you travel now by jumping/ taking weight on different body parts/ rolling actions, whilst maintaining movement?	Look for smooth links between movements, children working at the same time, sharing all the apparatus and the surrounding floorspace.
(b) Choose an area of your apparatus and join together 3 or 4 movements of your choice to show *travelling.*	Build in ideas of *control levels, speed, directions* and *quality of* performance. Use a demonstration per group to highlight and consolidate the work.

Closing activity

Once the apparatus has been put away ask the class as individuals what is their best jump, their best roll, their best taking weight movement. Get them to show them to a partner.

Cool-down

Choose an activity from the suppleness bank.

Back in the classroom

Recap of the lesson's activities – engage the children in discussion of what they have done.

- 'How did you travel? Well?'
- 'Did you travel under control? Quietly?'
- 'What was the most difficult aspect of the lesson?'
- Identify areas of improvement for each child.
- Outline next week's session – the challenges ahead.

Evaluation

- Did the class work safely?
- Did the class answer the tasks set? Some of them/all of them?
- How *well* were the tasks answered?
- How effective was the teacher's role in all of this?
- What needs further consolidation/more practice next week?

Progression and extension ideas

- More practice on basic movements and actions, encouraging variety at the same time.
- Better linking movements on apparatus (increasing competence in making the end of one action flow smoothly into the following one).
- Practise and improve the quality of the skills chosen by individuals.
- Rotate the groups onto different sets, and differently constructed apparatus layouts.
- More complex sequence tasks set.
- More opportunity to plan, practise and perform.

Cross-curricular work

Art – Investigating and Making – Plan and make three-dimensional structures using various material and for a variety of purposes.

Task: Design and make a scaled down sized model of a new piece of equipment which could be used in your hall. It could be a box or a completely new idea for a piece of apparatus that could be used in future gymnastics sessions.

Key Stage 2
Activity: Gymnastics, 'Originality'

Aims of the lesson (Focus)

- To encourage originality and self-selection of basic movements and actions.
- To develop competence in applying floor movements to apparatus.
- To introduce children to the beginnings of more complex sequence work.

National Curriculum – relevance to End of Key Stage Descriptions and Programmes of Study

> 'Pupils find solutions, sometimes responding imaginatively, to the various challenges that they encounter in the different areas of activity. They practise, improve and refine performance, and repeat series of movements they have performed previously, with increasing control and accuracy. They work alone, in pairs and in groups, and as members of a team. They make simple judgements about their own and other's performance, and use this information effectively to improve the accuracy, quality and variety of their own performance. They sustain energetic activity over appropriate periods of time, and demonstrate that they understand what is happening to their bodies during exercise.'
>
> 'Pupils should be taught ... different means of turning, rolling, swinging, jumping, climbing, balancing and travelling on hands and feet, and how to adapt, practise and refine these actions, both on the floor and using apparatus ... to emphasise changes of shape, speed and direction through gymnastic actions ... to practise, refine and repeat a longer series of actions, making increasingly complex movement sequences, both on the floor and using apparatus.'

Health-related focus

National Curriculum statement: 'pupils should be taught how to sustain energetic activity over appropriate periods of time in a range of physical activities ... the short-term effects of exercise on the body'.

The lesson activities include movements which focus on work involving suppleness, some strength aspects and a degree of work requiring stamina. In addition there is a need to build into the activities work on balance, control and a sharpening of co-ordinating skills. In the teacher/class review of the session this could be discussed.

Preparation in the classroom

Teacher
Think about the content of the lesson, building on previous work and movement experience generally. Ensure that the apparatus to be used during the session is positioned around the edges of the working space for easy access.

Children
Think about which 3 jumps you do best – prepare to work on these actions as soon as you enter the workspace. How will you alter them when attempting them on different pieces of apparatus?

Warm-up	
Activity in the working space Pulse raising activity and general body mobilising (use the 'warm-up bank')	*Points to watch and questions to ask* Look for a high level of mobility and action from the whole class.

Skills learning/development activities

Floorwork	
Activity in the working space	*Points to watch and questions to ask*
Practise your 3 jumps. Practise taking weight on hands. Join/link one of each together, i.e. a jump, a roll, taking weight, in any order.	Observe, comment on response/quality/individual performance. Insist on quiet bodies when rolling, jumping, etc.
Recap – 3 rolls, 3 jumps. Join together one jump and one roll. Recap – taking weight on hands – 3 different ways.	Look for enhanced quality in the movements, particularly the control elements.
Link one way of taking weight on hands with either a jump or a roll.	Work towards smoother links between the end of one movement and the beginning of the next.
Apparatus work	
Establish groups to assemble and arrange apparatus; allow a degree of freedom in terms of linkage and placement.	Calm and controlled, safe and purposeful. Awareness of others.
Encourage a variety of different levels, and good spacing.	Check fixings/ensure safety aspects.
Tasks: As skills and confidence develop look for opportunities to use the apparatus to link movements increasingly more smoothly.	Highlight response to task. Pick out, through open comment, initiatives and individual interpretations.
Use the entire layout of the apparatus (including the surrounding floorspace) to find through discovery where links are possible. Ensure control in the movements.	Demonstrations: use good examples of linking movements.

Closing activity

Once the apparatus is returned to the places it is stored, in open space practise a different link to those previously done in the lesson, i.e. linking a jump or a roll with taking weight on hands. Can you do it slowly and/or quickly?

Cool-down

Choose an activity from the suppleness bank.

Back in the classroom

- Review the work covered. How 'good' was the quality?
- What particular skills need more work?
- What can we improve to ensure that the end of one movement/action becomes more naturally the beginning of the next?
- How did we feel (physically) doing the work today?
- How did we feel (mentally) doing it?

Evaluation

- Did the children achieve the lesson aims?
- Did all the children understand the tasks set during the session?
- What needs further consolidation?
- Did you promote opportunities for the children to *plan, practise* and *evaluate?*
- Does the feedback from the children on how they did in the lesson help you plan for the next/follow-up session?
- How hard did everybody work?
- Did the children enjoy the session? Did you?

Progression and extension ideas

- Further practise and consolidation of two-part sequences.
- More apparatus work focusing on linking different structures together at different angles, levels, and places.
- More complex sequences increasingly coming from self-selection.
- Encouraging and adding direction/speed/levels/variations into the work.

Cross-curricular work

English – Descriptive Writing skills.

Task: Write a descriptive account of your best sequence of movements, either on the floor or apparatus; describe in detail what it involved and how you performed it. Accompany this with a diagram or picture.

Outdoor and Adventurous Activities

Key Stage 1
Activity: Outdoor and Adventurous Activity

Aims of the lesson (Focus)

- To provide vigorous and satisfying exercise.
- To introduce the idea of using a simple map.
- To enable the children to become familiar with their own school environment.

National Curriculum – relevance to End of Key Stage Descriptions and Programmes of Study

This area is not a National Curriculum requirement at Key Stage 1.

Health-related focus

National Curriculum statement: 'pupils should be taught about the changes that occur to their bodies as they exercise ... to recognise the short-term effects of exercise on the body.'

This lesson will provide lots of running which will help to promote stamina. There is little stretching or strength work. The warm-up will need to take account of that.

Preparation in the classroom

Teacher
- Choose a 'fitness' word and use its letters for your clues.
- Have plans of field or playground ready and letter clues (or pictures). Example required?
- Think about which children might work together. Decide on role of classroom assistant(s) or parent helper(s).
- Make sure you know about any hazards on the site you've chosen.
- Place your 'clues' in appropriate places – at prominent features. Place them so that they are accessible to the children. Make sure each pair or group of children has pencil and card for recording letters or pictures from clues.

Children
- Look at plan of field or playground.
- Talk about the symbols you've used – trees, paths, grass areas, fences etc.
- Show the children how the letter or picture clues are marked on their map.
- Explain how you want the children to follow the map to "collect" the picture/letter clues.
- Get everyone to change into suitable clothes/footwear for running outside.
- Explain how the children will be running – ask them how they think they will feel.

Warm-up

Activity in the working space	*Points to watch and questions to ask*
Choose an activity from the suppleness bank.	Make sure all the children have shoes properly tied.

Skills learning/development activities	***Observation points***
Activity in the work space	*Points to watch and questions to ask*
You may want to look at the maps with the whole class and find or show them one clue so that they know the kind of thing to look for.	Make sure the children all have their maps the right way round to start with (orientating or setting the map).
Place the children at different points around the area (in twos or threes).	Make sure again all the maps are the right way round.
Tell the children this is a race to collect all the letter/picture clues around the area as marked on the map. Tell them how much time they have.	Make sure the children know the starting and finishing signal and where to meet at the end of the activity.
Start the activity (by blowing whistle or ringing bell).	Move around the area checking on children's progress. If there is a particular hazard on the site (pond, car park) keep it in view all the time.
Children run around the site using their maps to find the letter/picture clues.	
After the set time (15–20 minutes) sound the finishing signal.	Make sure all the children safely return to the finishing point.

Cool-down and back in the classroom

This will vary depending on the weather, time of year etc. If very warm the children will need simply to sit down in a shady place for a few minutes. On a colder day they will need to go back inside the classroom more quickly. After the children's initial excitement has subsided you can discuss the activity with them. A physical cool-down (like stretching or relaxation exercises) is probably not necessary.

Ask the children:

- What did we learn?
- How did you feel when you were running?
- Did you find all the clues?
- Did you find anything difficult e.g. about reading the map?
- What did you enjoy the most?
- Do the letters collected make a word?
- What does it mean?

Evaluation

- To what extent did the lesson provide vigorous activity for all the children?
- How will did the children understand the use of the maps?
- Were there any problems with organisation or safety?
- What do the children need to do next?

Progression and extension ideas

Introduce the ideas of direction – left, right, forward, back.
Do similar games that use directions as well as clues on a map.
Extend the idea of direction into the main compass points (N,S,E,W).
Play running games using instructions to run N,S,E,W.
You can also introduce pulse counting – 'When you run further what happens to your heartbeat?' 'Can you count how many beats from when I say go...?'

Cross-curricular work

English – Speaking and Listening. Discuss with the children the meaning of the word created by your letter/picture clues. (e.g. 'stamina' means being able to keep going ... why is that important? etc.)

Key Stage 2
Activity: Outdoor and Adventurous Activity (Orienteering)

Aims of the lesson (Focus)

- To provide vigorous and satisfying exercise.
- To enable children to develop some understanding of direction and distance.
- To enable the children to develop some understanding of intensity of exercise (pace of walking/running).

National Curriculum – relevance to End of Key Stage Descriptions and Programmes of Study

> 'Pupils perform outdoor and adventurous activities in one or more different environments ... they experience the challenges of a physical and problem solving nature, whilst working individually and with others ... and they develop the skills necessary for the activities undertaken.'
> 'Pupils respond readily to instructions ... recognise and follow relevant rules, codes, etiquette and safety procedures for different activities ... be mindful of others and the environment.'

Health-related focus

National Curriculum statement: 'pupils should be taught about the changes that occur to their bodies as they exercise ... and to recognise the short-term effects of exercise on the body.'

This lesson will involve some exercise to develop stamina but little for flexibility or strength, so other lessons in the week should compensate (in gymnastics or dance, for example).

Preparation in the classroom

Teacher

- Prepare enough sets of instructions for one between 2 or 3 pupils as required.
- Make sure you have enough SILVA compasses for 1 between 2 at least.
- Prepare durable 'markers'. (Plastic plates upside down with numbers marked or stuck inside/ underneath are ideal.) Set out your course before the lesson. You could get older pupils (or adult helpers) to do it for you. Remember to use 'children's sized paces' and remember pacings will be approximate.

Children

- Go through the idea of compass points (using a globe if necessary) and get the children to point to the main points NSEW NE, SW etc. until you are sure they understand.
- Show the children how to find main compass points using a SILVA compass.
- Show the children an instruction sheet in enlarged form (on OHP or chalkboard) and explain what they are going to do – navigating and pacing distances from point to point.

Warm-up

Activity in the working space	*Points to watch and questions to ask*
Use a running game (calling N.S.E.W.) to raise children's pulses and reinforce concept of navigation.	Keep children spaced out to avoid collisions.

Skills learning/development activities

Activity in the working space
Get the children together and show them how the markers are placed around the playground or field.
Place two children at each marker and let them look (lifting up the plate) to see which it is.
Then ask them to find their way to the next following the instructions on the sheet (e.g. 3 → 4: 20 paces East).
After a few minutes (say, when you are sure each pair has got the idea and found 3 markers) get them all to move to a different marker.
From there get them to find all the other markers in turn and make this a race.
The children will now be pacing very quickly to get quickly to the markers and the exercise will be more strenuous.
If the children do this quickly (and if there is time) give them a set of random numbers (4 or 6 to each pair) and get them to write down the directions (bearings) and distances to these.

Points to watch and questions to ask
Ensure that the children are using their compasses to check that they are moving towards the current marker, and that they are actually pacing the distance. Some children will quickly find short cuts, especially if your markers are quite close together

Cool-down

This will depend on the weather and the distances covered by your course. If the distances were large enough to get the children breathless, they will need just to sit down and recover. This can be a good time for 'debriefing'.

Back in the classroom

Check all the children fully understand main compass points.
Ask:

- How did you feel when you were running fast? Walking?
- How much distance did you cover – can you work it out?
- Can you draw your own plan of the playground/field?

Evaluation

- To what extent were all the children active for the whole lesson?
- How well did the children judge distance and direction?
- Were all the children able to tolerate the exertion of the lesson?
- How could you make this activity more challenging?
- What do the children need to do next?

Progression and extension ideas

- Take the children to a local park or open land.
- Extend pacing activities over longer distances.
- Set challenges for children to walk up hills – how many paces can you walk up before you're out of breath? How many stops did we make on the way up?
- Set directional walking/pacing tasks to visible landmarks (tall tree, house, telegraph pole, etc.)
- At school: let the children devise and plan their own orienteering courses.

Cross-curricular work

Geography (Geographical Skills):
- Follow a route using a plan
- Make a map of a short route showing features in the correct order.

Task: Ask the children to draw a simple map showing the route they took during the lesson.

Key Stage 2 (age 10–11)
Activity: Outdoor and Adventurous Activity, Trust, Co-operation and Challenge

Aims of the lesson (Focus)

- To provide challenge and opportunities for co-operative work.
- To develop basic climbing skills and confidence at controlled heights.
- To develop physical trust.

National Curriculum – relevance to End of Key Stage Descriptions and Programmes of Study

> 'Pupils perform outdoor and adventurous activities in one or more different environments ... they experience the challenges of a physical and problem solving nature, whilst working individually and with others ... and they develop the skills necessary for the activities undertaken.'
> 'Pupils respond readily to instructions ... learn how to lift, carry, place and use equipment safely ... recognise and follow relevant rules and safety procedures for different activities ... be mindful of others.'

Health-related focus

National Curriculum statement: 'pupils should be taught about the changes that occur to their bodies as they exercise ... to recognise the short-term effects of exercise on the body.'

This lesson will involve lots of bending, stretching, reaching, pulling and pushing – quite good therefore for suppleness and strength. The warm-up will need to be quite vigorous to provide some exercise to promote stamina.

Preparation in the classroom

Teacher
- Have clear idea of apparatus to be used and challenges to be set.
- Think through possible composition of groups (or methods of selection)
- Think through safety issues and need for additional adult help (parents or classroom assistants)
- Make sure all apparatus and equipment is accessible and ready to use.
- Be ready in appropriate clothing and footwear as positive role model.

Children
- Discuss nature of activity including physical challenge, co-operation. Teacher needs to emphasise safety measures if children don't raise safety issues.
- Teacher needs to emphasise the importance of thinking about other people's safety.
- Make sure all the children are appropriately dressed – T-shirts and shorts would be ideal, and bare feet will be safer than shoes for climbing on apparatus.

Warm-up

Activity in the working space	*Points to watch and questions to ask*
A running/chasing game to get children warm and raise pulse rates, followed by general mobilising exercise.	Make sure all the children are warm and have stretched properly, but sit them down calmly before beginning the challenge.

Skills learning/development activities

Activity in the working space

Set up a number of challenges using gymnastics equipment to simulate challenges to be found in the hills and mountains. For example, an inclined bench up to the cave:

- Southampton frame with a plank or bar across to the other frame, and another bench or plank down.
- Ropes hanging down.
- Three stools linked by planks to form an L-shaped pathway.
- A series of stools and vaulting horses to form a low tunnel.

The idea is that the children must avoid touching designated areas e.g. the floor, the ropes, the sides of the frame. They therefore need to take great care in their movements.

Set the children to explore these challenges individually, explaining that they represent, say, a climb to a cliff top and across a narrow ledge weaving in and out of trees, stepping-stones or logs across a river.

Once all the children have attempted each of the challenges, bring them together and discuss what is involved – the need not to touch the frame when crawling through etc.

Points to watch and questions to ask

You can set the height or difficulty of the challenges according to the experience and capability of the children.

Skill performance or game

Activity in the working space

Divide the children into groups of 3 and set a range of tasks.

1. Each group has to carry a gym mat through or over each of the challenges or obstacles.
2. Each member of the group is blindfolded in turn and has to be led through or over each of the challenges or obstacles.
3. Each group has to carry a heavy object (e.g. a plank, a bench or chair) over or through selected challenges.

Points to watch and questions to ask

You may decide to ask the children to form their own groups – be aware of trying to ensure a mix of abilities and of girls and boys.

Allow plenty of time for encouragement and careful 'inching along' by the blindfolded person who is guided and/or physically led by the other two team members.

Be very aware of safety here and allow lots of time for preparation and discussion.

Cool-down

The children will be excited so a relaxation activity will be more important than a physical cool-down. A visualisation exercise would be appropriate.

Back in the classroom

Discuss the activity:
- What did you enjoy?
- What did you learn?
- What was difficult?
- Why was it difficult?
- Did you do anything you thought you couldn't do?

If video was used to record the activities, this could be a useful and additional focus for the discussion.

Evaluation

- How effective were the challenges you chose?
- Were all the children fully involved and able to play different roles?
- Was there sufficient strenuous exercise in the session?
- Were all the children able to co-operate fully? Were all the children aware of safety issues?
- Which aspects of the session could be reinforced?
- Which could be developed further?

Progression and extension ideas

- Change the composition of groups to allow others to take leadership roles.
- Increase height of challenges (while maintaining careful attention to safety).
- Use upside-down bench as balance beam for 'river crossings'.
- Send children around the course (or to tackle specific challenges) in teams of 3 or 4 roped together.
- Introduce competitive timing element – time added on for touching obstacles (Extra attention to safety needed if competition introduced).
- Adapt activities to apparatus outside (ropes, rubber tyres, logs, barrels, etc.).
- Pupils plan their own circuit including safety elements.

Cross-curricular work

- PSHE (Trust, co-operation, responding to challenges).
- Technology (identification of need, problem solving, apparatus design and building).
- Mathematics (height, weight, distance ...).
- Geography (discussion of rivers, gorges, cliffs, rocky shores, map and compass skills).
- English (speaking and listening, writing for a variety or purposes).

Swimming

Key Stage 1
Activity: Swimming

Aims of the lesson (Focus)

- To develop confidence in the water.
- To involve the children in enjoyable activities and to introduce the concept of water resistance.
- To teach children the prone position and to develop their confidence in achieving that position and feeling safe in the water.

National Curriculum – relevance to End of Key Stage Descriptions and Programmes of Study

'Pupils plan and perform simple skills safely, and show control in linking actions together. They improve their performance through practising their skills, working alone and with a partner. They talk about what they and others have done, and are able to make simple judgements. They recognise and describe the changes that happen to their bodies during exercise.'
'Pupils should be taught ... to swim unaided, competently and safely, for at least 25 metres ... to develop confidence in water, and how to rest, float and adopt support positions ... a variety of means of propulsion using either arms or legs or both, and how to develop effective and efficient swimming strokes on the front and the back ... the principles and skills of water safety and survival.'

Health-related focus

- Stretching, stamina and resistance activities improving strength.
- These units will help develop children's confidence, their self-esteem and will teach them the association between effort and reward.
- The lessons will increase awareness of hygiene generally and pool hygiene specifically.

Preparation in the classroom

Teacher
Is the equipment necessary for the lesson on the pool side (floats, arm-bands etc)?
Do the children know how to enter the pool area and the water itself safely?
Will the children shower, walk through footbath and enter the teaching area in a controlled manner?
Are there ropes etc. ready to designate different areas for children at different stages of learning?
Is the supervision of changing for both sexes organised?

Children
When children first enter the swimming area they should sit if possible away from the water.
If this not feasible then on the side of the pool. They should *never* enter the pool area without an adult in attendance.
Ask the children what they are going to be doing.

Warm-up	
Activity in the working space As pool time is at a premium this should take place in the water and should relate to the main activities of the lesson.	*Points to watch and questions to ask* Children may be excited by the prospect of their swimming lesson. The teacher should channel the energy in a controlled manner for the first few minutes and set the pattern for the session.

Skills learning/development activities	
Activity in the working space First: Children pair off; then in pairs (holds onto bar and watches the other) walking anywhere (in roped area) sliding feet on the bottom of the pool. Then vary style of walking, skating, sideways, turning etc. Ask all children to cup hands and wash face and head. Use floats or light balls and in pairs blow or push object to partner using hands, then elbows, then head, nose etc. Class to put on arm bands and walk around pool getting used to feeling the arms floating, shoulders under water. Lift feet off pool floor with small jumps, higher jumps, cup hands and use for balance/control.	*Points to watch and questions to ask* Is the pupil confident? Comfortable? Is she or he concentrating on the activity or her or his safety? Fear or participation? Reassurance for some individuals? Are children comfortable with the activity? Don't rub eyes', 'blow out of your nose when under water' etc. If arm bands are being used, are they fitted correctly and properly inflated? The temporary role of arm bands should be made clear.

Skill performance or game	
Exercises (to music if possible) in water, e.g. arm swinging, shoulder raises, leg kicking, arm stretching/pushing waist and hip circles, jumping/running on the spot to the rhythm. End session, climb out in orderly manner – shower.	Comfortable distance between pupils. Are all pupils clearly in view and are they still in pairs?

Back in the classroom

Ask the children:
- How did they feel?
- Which part did they enjoy most?'
- What do you (and they)think they could improve on?'

Emphasise they will feel less breathless the more they get used to regular swimming.

Evaluation

- Did all pupils learn something?
- Did each pupil develop their confidence and improve their performance?
- Have you recorded what happened in the lesson?
- Who are the pupils who need further confidence building practices?
- Are pupils who are developing most quickly being challenged?
- Was the session completely safe?
- Is it possible to split the class into different groups to more effectively cater for the range of abilities?

Progression and extension ideas

- Gliding. Hold onto side/bar? Swing into prone position? Leg kicking, kicking towards side from 1 metre. Increase distance.
- Floats instead of arm bands. Practise prone, supine positions in water. Move to full extension of arms.
- Work towards gliding *away* from side with face in water to standing up position. Progress to leg kick with float held in front.
- Add leg kick and arm movements as confidence grows.
- Add breathing practice (on one side only) as stamina develops. Work towards a whole width (legs and arms) with one breath taken halfway.

Cross-curricular work

English AT1 (Speaking and Listening) AT3 (Writing).
Task: talk about words which make you think about water, e.g. 'splish, splosh, gurgle'. Read a poem with the children about water (streams, the sea etc.). Ask the children to write their own water words and illustrate them.

Key Stage 1/2
Activity: Swimming improvers. Theme: Breast stroke arm action

Aims of the lesson

- To improve propulsion through the water.
- To improve ankle flexibility.
- To improve swimming endurance through use of a stronger leg kick action.

National Curriculum – relevance to End of Key Stage Descriptions and Programmes of Study

> 'Pupils find solutions, sometimes responding imaginatively, to the various challenges that they encounter in the different areas of activity ... they practise, improve and refine performance, and repeat series of movements they have performed previously, with increasing control and accuracy .... They work safely alone, in pairs and in groups, and as members of a team .... They make simple judgements about their own and others' performance, and use this information effectively to improve the accuracy, quality and variety of their own performance ... they sustain energetic activity over appropriate periods of time, and demonstrate that they understand what is happening to their bodies during exercise.'
> 'Pupils should be taught ... to swim unaided, competently and safely, for at least 25 metres ... to develop confidence in water, and how to rest, float and adopt support positions ... a variety of means of propulsion using either arms or legs or both, and how to develop effective and efficient swimming strokes on the front and the back ... the principles and skills of water safety and survival.'

Health-related focus

National Curriculum statement: 'Throughout the key stage, pupils should be taught ... how to sustain energetic activity over appropriate periods of time in a range of physical activities ... the short-term effects of exercise on the body.'
This session will involve a lot of work on leg flexibility, co-ordination and stamina.

Preparation in the classroom

Teacher
- Are the children in the correct groups for learning this particular stroke?
- Is any equipment ready?
- Have the pupils learnt and progressed throughout previous sessions, and are they ready for more explicit work to improve all-round technique?

Children
- Are the children aware of their own level of ability?
- Do all children know how to identify faults and do they have the ability to correct mistakes?
- Are they capable of communicating with their partners about their partners' technique?
- Are they prepared to work hard to improve their own individual performance?

Warm-up	
Activity in the working space	*Points to watch and questions to ask*
Enter the water safely and swim four widths of your favourite stroke(s).	Keep the children 'on task' – no break permitted in the four widths.

Skills learning/ development activities	
1. Stand in the water, resting chin on surface, draw large circles with your hands as you lean forwards – arms extended.	Look for palms facing down and hands pressing outwards and back. Bring arms down, drop the elbows at a point in front of the shoulders. Bring the arms together until the palms meet. Slide hands forwards and return to the extended position.
2. Practise the arm action as you walk in shallow water.	The arms are moved in a downward, outward and backward direction initially, to the point when the hands are just in front of the shoulder line and a right angle is formed between the arms.
3. Perform the full stroke using floats – hold the float between the thighs.	Keep the action in front of the shoulders. The downward and backward pressure of the arms propels the body forward – this aids breathing by raising the head and the chest.
4. Practise without aids when confident.	Swim widths concentrating on arm propulsion.
5. Concluding activity: In pairs – swim as quietly as possible, no splash from hands or feet.	Praise and comment on good performance and notable improvements.

Evaluation

- How many children have improved their technique?
- What were the common faults? How can they be rectified?
- What extra practice is needed next session and for which individuals?
- Did individuals that showed major faults become aware of what they need to improve?
- Do some children perform at an advanced level?
- Are you, as the teacher, recording childrens' progress effectively? How and where?

Progression and extension ideas

- Pupils set themselves improvement targets.
- Practice of breathing and timing while performing the breast stroke.
- Further leg and arm action practise through push and glide work.

Cross-curricular work

Science – Physical Processes – Forces and motion – methods of propulsion; floating and sinking principles.
Design & Technology – Designing and making skill /Knowledge and understanding – using appropriate materials (e.g. pipe cleaners, pins, etc.) design and make your own manikin which can illustrate effectively body actions for swimming.

Key Stage 1/2
Activity: Swimming improvers. Theme: Leg propulsion

Aims of the lesson

- To improve propulsion through the water.
- To improve ankle flexibility.
- To improve swimming endurance through use of a stronger leg kick action.

National Curriculum – relevance to End of Key Stage Descriptions and Programmes of Study

'Pupils find solutions, sometimes responding imaginatively, to the various challenges that they encounter in the different areas of activity ... they practise, improve and refine performance, and repeat series of movements they have performed previously, with increasing control and accuracy .... They work safely alone, in pairs and in groups, and as members of a team ... They make simple judgements about their own and others' performance, and use this information effectively to improve the accuracy, quality and variety of their own performance .... they sustain energetic activity over appropriate periods of time, and demonstrate that they understand what is happening to their bodies during exercise.'
'Pupils should be taught ... to swim unaided, competently and safely, for at least 25 metres ... to develop confidence in water, and how to rest, float and adopt support positions ... a variety of means of propulsion using either arms or legs or both, and how to develop effective and efficient swimming strokes on the front and the back ... the principles and skills of water safety and survival.'

Health-related focus

National Curriculum statement: 'Throughout the key stage, pupils should be taught ... how to sustain energetic activity over appropriate periods of time in a range of physical activities ... the short-term effects of exercise on the body.'
This session will involve a lot of work on leg flexibility, co-ordination and stamina.

Preparation in the classroom

Teacher
- Are the children in the correct groups for learning this particular stroke? Equipment ready?
- Have the pupils learnt and progressed throughout this visit to an improved level of competence?

Children
- Do children know their own level of ability? Do all children know how to identify faults and do they have the ability to correct mistakes?
- Are they capable of communicating with their partners about their partners' technique?

Warm-up

Activity in the working space	*Points to watch and questions to ask*
Enter the water under control and using your preferred stroke, swim from the side of the pool for one minute.	Look out for pupils who demonstrate sound leg kick technique for demonstration purposes late in the session.

Skills learning/ development activities	
1. Using a float at arm's length, experiment with different ways of using the legs for propulsion.	Look for strength of leg action; use a couple of demonstrators to illustrate the need for this.
2. Holding a float swim widths using front crawl leg action. Concentrate on these actions as widths are swum.	The upkick comes initially from the hip – and during this the leg is extended almost straight, enabling the sole of the foot and the back of the leg to 'press' against the water and provide propulsion. In the downward movement the instep and outer areas of the extended foot push downwards and outwards, providing forward movement. Therefore: 'swing the legs from the hips, keep the ankles loose, point the toes, keep the legs close together, and aim for a continuous action.'
3. Swim widths of back crawl holding a float either at arm's length in front, at arm's length above the head, behind the head, or on the chest. Concentrate on leg propulsion as widths of back crawl are swum.	The upkick provides propulsion, as before, beginning from the hip, and travelling through a slightly bent knee and passes to the foot which should be fully extended and slightly turned in. The extension of the knee causes a whipping action of the foot driving the water upward and backward. (Expect to see different levels of performance since the amount of push exerted depends on the size of the foot, the strength of leg muscles and the amount of individual ankle flexibility.) Therefore: 'swing the legs from the hips, make the legs long, point the toes, and stress the upkick.'
4. Concluding activity: Divide into teams (of 4) – swim in relay, using different leg kick actions every time a team member completes a length.	Monitor, praise, and if time use one team to demonstrate a good example.

Evaluation

- How many children have improved their technique?
- Do some children perform at an advanced level?
- What extra practice is needed next session and for which individuals?
- Did individuals that showed major faults become aware of what they need to improve?

Are you, as the teacher, recording childrens' progress effectively?

Progression and extension ideas

- Stroke improvement sessions
- Practice of breast stroke leg action
- Further leg action practice through treading water exercises, and sculling activities.

Cross-curricular work

Safety around water. Emergency routine in case of accident. Basic life saving/resuscitation introduction.

Science – methods of propulsion; how a water jet works; how mammals propel themselves through water.

Example

Frameworks for Planning a Unit of Work

Area of Activity: Gymnastics KS1

Year: One Key Stage: One Time (no of lessons): 6 sessions (35 mins approx) Title of unit: Development of different ways of travelling
Cross-Curricular elements: English – Vocabulary/Language Maths – Shapes/Size/Direction

Lesson Structure	**Lesson 1** Travelling using feet	**Lesson 2** Travelling using hands and feet	**Lesson 3** Travelling using hands and feet	**Lesson 4** Travelling using body, front/back	**Lesson 5** Travelling on body surfaces	**Lesson 6** Travelling and joining movements
Introduction	Find a space, walk around room without touching anyone. Musical statues. Stop on command. Run around in space. Stop on command. Musical statues. Repeat. Jumping around room. Demonstrations from some of the class. Discuss. Try these ways.	Find a space and walk around the room in different directions. On command just move forwards then backwards and sideways. Then move using any way. On hands and feet, keep hands still and move both feet at once to a different spot (springing).	In a space travel around on their feet in some way. Then just on the spot. Then use both hands and feet to travel around the room. Then on the spot. Choose and move in different directions, and at different speeds.	In a space travel on front. As many different ways. Then on backs. Make shapes that are round, then long and then thin. After each shape demonstrations by individuals and groups	In a space travel around room using all different body parts big, then small. Change direction and speeds quick and slow. Different levels – high and low movements.	Travelling around room practising methods from previous weeks. Continuous teacher input so that they join together into the next movements. Include travelling on feet, hands and other body parts.
Floorwork	Travel by hopping on left leg, then right. Skipping. Stopping on commands – moving on the spot during these same ways of travel. Emphasis on moving around quickly, then slowly. Individuals give demonstrations.	Bend down on floor on hands and feet. Crawl around room in spaces. In a space with hands static, lift one leg up, then the other. Both at the same time. Bunnyhops around room. Stop on on command. Individuals demonstrating movements.	Emphasis on travelling on feet quickly, in different directions, then slow movements. Same aspect using hands and feet. Emphasis on travelling and big and small shapes, feet first, then hands and feet together. Demonstrations.	Emphasis on travelling front and back, big shapes then small ones. Pulling along floor, rolling over pushing themselves over. Pairs taking it in turns to make a shape practised previously. Partner copies.	Concentration on timing of movements quickly and slowly. Using all different body parts. Emphasis on high and low movements in different directions.	Emphasis on joining together actions. On command they have to change another movement joining it somehow, until the next command in which they change to something else different.
Apparatus	Travelling around slowly, weaving in and over hoops and low skittles/cones. Walking at first, not touching anyone. Change to skipping then jumping (still slowly). Choose any method tried and get around/over as many objects as possible, still slowly.	Travel around room, across mats and benches. When on a mat you have to bunny-hop across it and hoops you crawl around. Each time you get to a new object they have to travel in a different method from the last one.	Using benches and mats travel around and explore big movements, then small. Have to make different movements around lower object using feet/feet and hands. Demonstrations from individuals.	Travelling around and onto equipment, under cones across mats and benches, slowly. Put into pairs and one follows and copies partner, swap over. Have to use all equipment. Demonstration by pairs.	Travelling around and onto equipment using all body parts, slowly then quickly. Include all actions experienced in previous lessons. Over benches, mats, under skittles and cones etc. Copy a partner. Pairs show some examples of things they have been doing.	Using benches, mats, hoops, skittles and cones as last week practise and repeat three movements that join together. Demonstrations. Partners practise and repeat three movements also. Perform to class.
Conclusion	Demonstrations by individuals. Traffic lights game.	Demonstrations. Musical statues (travelling around on hands and feet).	With a partner, travel around the room skipping, change movements on command.	Travelling around room on front, on command roll over and travel on back.	Travelling around room in high movements, on command low movements different each time.	Game of 'Simon Says'. e.g. 'Simon says move around on your hands and feet'.

Resources needed:	**End of key stage descriptions:**	**Criteria for assessing attainment:**
Hoops, Skittles, Cones, Mats, Ropes, Benches, Planks, Nesting Tables.	Plan and perform a range of simple actions and linked movements to given stimuli	A class summary sheet, transferred to individual summary sheets. Children are able to transfer their body weight confidently. They explore ways of travelling with and without apparatus.
General requirements across all key stages:	**POS (general) for each key stage:**	**POS (activity specific):**
Plan and perform simple actions and linked ones in response to a task – safely. Practise and improve performance Describe what they are doing Recognise the effects of physical activity on their bodies.	Experience basic actions of travel, turning, jumping, balancing, taking weight on hands etc. Be given opportunity to practise and improve Linked actions/movements together Be taught safety elements of using simple apparatus	Experience many ways of performing the basic actions of travelling. Be given opportunity to link together a series of actions on the floor and be able to repeat them.

Gymnastics KS1: Unit of Work – 'Joining Movements' 6 x 35 minute lessons

	Lesson 1	Lesson 2	Lesson 3	Lesson 4	Lesson 5	Lesson 6
Warm-up	Travel near the floor in different directions, at different speeds, on different body parts.	In free space practise start and finish positions – build-in a 3-second pause in each – link with a travel; link with a jumping action.	Free use of space – on commands STOP and 1. Practise a favourite jump; 2. Practise a weight on hands action. Alternate/repeat.	Response work: STOP, GO, FREEZE, JUMP, ROLL, BALANCE, WEIGHT ON HANDS, etc.	Walk freely – jog – run faster – avoid others. Repeat – practise changes of speed, pace, turns.	Stretches for suppleness; mix-up with 'dynamic' actions, e.g. short sprints, jumps, etc.
Floorwork	Practise ways of rolling/jumping Practise taking weight momentarily on hands, always returning to feet. Demonstrations.	Weight on hands – revision and further practice. Join up with a start/finish position. Add a jump. Small group demonstrations.	Balance work: Practise balancing on combinations of different body parts – head, hands, feet, hips, back, side, etc. Develop to 3-point balances/ 2-point balances Demonstrations – individual.	Mat work in pairs: alternately roll lengthwise – do it in a different way roll widthwise/ corner to corner. Add a start/finish.	Pairs on mats – practise changing the speed of your favourite rolling actions (across mats lengthwise, widthwise, diagonally). Join 2 together that show different speeds.	Practise selected favourite movements – jumps, balances, rolls, weight on hands – link together the best two. Individual demonstrations.
Apparatus	Groups of 4: Allocate areas and apparatus, and assemble. Set task: Work on, around, over, under, up, down, across, in-between, by travelling, jumping, rolling and weight on hands movements. Group demonstrations.	Groups of 4: As previous week erect allotted apparatus and rotate round to next 'set'. Practise: 1. Places to get on and off the apparatus. 2. Places where jumps, and weight on hands actions can be linked. 3. Add start/finish positions. 4. Show the sequence.	Groups of 5 or 6 – allocate specific apparatus. Tasks: 1. Move freely on the apparatus finding places to take up and hold balance positions; 2. Places where 3 and 2 point balances can be performed. Get groups to demonstrate in their 5's or 6's.	Set up as last week, but allow the class to have use of and freedom of all the apparatus in the hall. Tasks: 1. Find different entry points onto the apparatus and different exit points. 2. Link with rolling actions on different apparatus.	Groups of 5 or 6: allocate one bench, one plank, two mats. Tasks: 1. Alternate slow and faster rolling actions, with an emphasis on ***control***. 2. Choose either a balance or a jump, and add it to the roll. (Add start/finish positions). Demonstrations.	Free use of the whole apparatus: select an area to work in, and practise joining together movements on and around the apparatus, working particularly on control. Add changes of speed to the actions, and work at differing levels.
Conclusion	Practise favourite jumping actions, bend knees on take-off and landings.	Discuss the activities with the class, 'what do we need to work on in the next session?'	Practise your favourite balance – try to hold it for a count of 3 seconds. Repeat. Demonstrations.	Discuss with the class the work covered today – what could be improved in the next session?	Repeat last task using the floor-space only. Demonstrations.	Demonstrations Summarise efforts through group discussion.

Resources	**Assessment:**
Floorspace; apparatus: mats (minimum of one between two) nesting tables, trestles, agility table, benches, planks, stools, bar-box, section box, climbing-frame, ropes, etc.	Have the class widened their vocabulary of movement? Are they able to work collaboratively, share space and equipment? Are the skills of lifting and carrying apparatus developing in a sound, safe way? Do they implement ideas of their own when constructing apparatus pathways? Is there an understanding of how the end of one movement becomes the beginning of the next when joining movements/starting sequences? Is there a sense of timing developing – do they know what a balance held for 3 seconds 'feels' like? Were all children extended in their work, all abilities stretched within tasks set? Was opportunity given for all to share and show their ideas?

Gymnastics Curriculum Unit: KS2 Main Theme: Balance

LESSON	INTRODUCTION	FLOORWORK	APPARATUS	FLOORWORK	RELATIONSHIPS
1. Large body parts	Running and stopping to freeze and hold. Run a few steps jump and land, hold balance.	Explore balancing on a variety of different body parts. e.g. front, back, side, hips. Holding same base experiment changing body shape.	Practise balancing on low level apparatus on large body parts. Choose two balances repeat them try to change body shape.	Make a sequence of three balances making sure that they flow from one to the other.	Individual
2. Small body parts	Move about the hall and on a signal balance using different parts of the body and different ways. Hold the balance for 3 seconds.	Explore balancing on different body parts on the floor. 3,2,1 point balances. Experimenting with different support bases over large and small areas.	Practise moving onto apparatus and balancing on a variety of small body parts. Choose a balance on a large body part and a small body part and travel between them.	Choose three different balances on different body parts. Practise balancing.	Individual
3. Shape	Run around gym and on command, jump: – up to tuck jump – long to stretch jump – wide to star	Explore stretched/tucked balance shapes around different body parts – contracted around a part e.g. stomach – extended – part extended and part contracted	Find different ways of balancing on different parts of the apparatus, holding a stretched, tucked or wide balance based around different body part. Travel onto apparatus and balance.	Devise a pattern of three balances showing tucked, stretched and wide shapes moving between each balance. Perform a roll-balance-roll-balance	Individual Individuals and pairs
4. Moving into and out of a balance	Move around gym and respond to commands left – touch floor with left hand right – touch floor with right hand jump – show a shape	Revise the different parts of the body for balancing. Try different ways of moving into a balance: standing, roll, jump. Hold a balance and roll out of it. Find different ways of leaving a balance.	Travel-balance incorporate mounting and dismounting using different parts of the body.	using two different rolls/balances. Teach your sequence to a partner and try to learn theirs.	
5. Partners	Follow a partner around gym and copy exactly what they do. Repeat but change roles. Theme: 'different types of balance.'	Practise one balance so partner can jump over. Practise one balance so partner can go under without contact.	Get onto apparatus from different starting points and arrive on apparatus at same time. End with exiting at different times. One balances so partner can go over or go under.	Work out a sequence of three balances so that you alternatively balance and get over or under a partner's balance.	Pairs
6. Performance	Travel using jumping, rolling, moving onto hands and feet varying body shapes.	Make up a sequence with a partner to include a balance, jump, roll, movement on hands/feet. Think about start/end of sequence. Perform sequence.	Using the floor and apparatus work with a partner to produce a sequence. Think about using different body parts, shapes, movement into and out of a balance, moving in a variety of ways.	Choose, practise and refine a sequence with a partner that you like. Perform sequence.	Pairs.

Cross-Curricular Links Health education Safety Personal and social skills Problem solving	**End Of Key Stage Descriptions** – Find solutions/respond imaginatively to challenges – Repeat movements with control and accuracy – Work safely alone and in pairs – Make judgements about performances to improve – Sustain activity	**POS (General)** – How to sustain energetic activity over periods of time – short-term effects of exercise on the body	**POS (Activity Specific)** (a) different means of turning, rolling, jumping – travelling on hands and how to adapt, practise and refine these (b) emphasise changes of shape, speed, direction (c) practise, refine, repeat series of actions on floor and apparatus
Resources Mats, benches, box, ropes, wall bars, nesting tables, planks	**General Requirements** – To be physically active, adopt good posture – Develop flexibility/muscular strength – Develop positive attitudes – Ensure safe practice	**Criteria For Assessment** – Class working safely – control – Class answering task – listening, responding – Quality produced in response to task – Response to teaching – Ability to work with others	– Accuracy of movement – Evidence of good design – Imaginative performance – Ability to do more than one thing at a time – Sustained participation

Area of Activity: GAMES, KS1

Year: One Key Stage: One Time (no of lessons): 6 sessions (35 mins approx) Title of unit: Development of different ways of travelling, sending and receiving skills
Cross-Curricular elements: English – Vocabulary/Language Maths – Shapes/Size/Direction

Lesson Structure	**Lesson 1** Travelling/sending	**Lesson 2** Rolling/pushing	**Lesson 3** Throwing/catching	**Lesson 4** Hitting/striking	**Lesson 5** Simple games	**Lesson 6** Stations Session
Introduction	Run, travel in own space, stop on command. Game of traffic lights. Pick up a bean bag, put on ground, different ways of jumping over it. Demonstrate to others.	Running in a space with beanbag. Place in space, visit as many as you can, until stop command. Travelling at different speeds, slow and fast. Demonstrate to others.	Travelling in different ways. In a space. Traffic lights. Collect a bean bag. How many ways can you pass it around your body? Continue by travelling around room as well as moving around the body.	Travelling around room, weaving around hoops, not to touch, in different ways. Walk at first, jumping etc. Travelling around and visit as many hoops as possible. Stop inside one on command (one each).	Travelling around with ball when stop command given bounce once. How many bounces can I do before I say stop in 15 seconds? How many times can you pass it around your body?	4 groups and 4 stations. One game to weave in and out of 6 hoops balancing bean bag on hand. One game to make a line in the group. How many times can they throw a beanbag to end person of line and roll back. Throw forwards and roll the other way. One game to travel in different ways. Throw a bean bag in a hoop, next person gets it. Repeat. One game to aim and throw three bean bags at quoits then at hoops. Collects. Alternates in group.Each group demonstrates one station at end of first rotation.
Development	Run in between bean bags. Stop on command. Get a quoit. Touch bean bags with this. Go to own bean bag. Jump over, turn and aim quoit at it. Repeat. Put quoit away. Running with bag, stop, change with friend.	Collect a quoit. Stand near and push bean bag along floor towards quoit to try to hit it. Repeat. Change the pushing hand. Change distance from quoit. Pushing at different speeds.	Collect a ball. Try moving around body also. Demonstrations. Using ball throw and catch in air. Do same walking around, in a space. Stand still, throw to nearest person. Change to a bean bag.	Collect a bean bag. Using both hands, stand near hoop and try to hit the hoop. Collect and try again. Collect a ball, throw underarm to inside of hoop, move away further to make difficult. Roll ball to hoop.	Travelling around hoops bouncing ball on command. How many hoops can you visit and roll into the middle of? How many hoops can you visit and hit and catch in the middle?	
Conclusion	Balance bean bag on hand, different ways. Travel around in different ways in room.	Travel around the space with the bag. Send bag to quoit, aim, collect. Repeat. Continue to other quoits around room. Travel around pushing and aiming bags. How many can you hit? Discuss.	In pairs, throw bean bags to partner, changing the distance to make it more difficult. Incorporate work from last lesson, rolling, pushing to partner. Discuss.	Demonstrate to others. Travel around with ball in both hands, when get to hoop, hit in centre and catch. Repeat and try other hoops. Discuss.	With a partner, bounce five times and throw to partner who catches and repeats. How many times can you swap the ball before the stop command: Rolling to partner quickly and slowly. Demonstrate and discuss.	

Resources needed:	**End of key stage descriptions:**	**Criteria for assessing attainment:**
Bean bags, quoits, size 3/4 balls, hoops, plastic markers, chalk, feet markers.	To practise and improve their performance.	A class summary sheet, transferred to individual summary sheets
General requirements across all key stages: Develop skills of running, jumping, use of space etc. by – experimenting individually – using equipment to send away, receive, hit, strike, aim at a target – exchange with a partner, group – activities of beating your own score, how quickly? How many times? How many different ways?	**POS (general) for each key stage:** To be encouraged to practise and perform simple skills. To follow safety requirements, including lifting, carrying and moving equipment	**POS (activity specific):** To experience using a variety of games equipment, where appropriate. To experience practice and develop a variety of ways of sending, rolling, and travelling with a ball and other equipment.

Gymnastics KS2: Unit of Work – 'Ball handling and Invasion Games'   6 x 40 minute lessons

	Lesson 1	Lesson 2	Lesson 3	Lesson 4	Lesson 5	Lesson 6
Warm-up	6 Groups: Relay over 10 metres – turn at cone and transfer ball to next runner (throw, give, pass, etc.).	Repeat 'Zig-Zag' Game from last session – emphasise control, organisation and speed of reaction.	Individual footwork skills – on command stop/start, run along different pathways. Teach the pivot turn on right and left foot.	In areas of 8 x 8 and groups of 4, practise pass and receive using pivoting skills to move ball clockwise and anti-clockwise. How fast can you do it without losing control?	Use whole area – ball between each pair – on signal pass and move skills as whole group. On second whistle which pairs can still retain possession. Repeat.	Small ball each practise spinning the ball, using 2 hands, left hand only, right hand only. Can you spin the ball away from you and make it return? (Try to imagine you are opening a door handle with the ball.)
Skills work	Ball each – practise catching and throwing skills, initially in a personal space, then while moving. Change ball with somebody who has been working with a different size/shape, etc. Repeat.	In 2's across appropriate distances, practise catching and throwing skills – emphasise accuracy, control and variety. Build in a travelling/pass and move development. Set a time challenge – 'how many successful passes can you make in the next 30 seconds ...' etc.	In 3's practise two-handed passing skills: Bucket, chest, bounce, overhead. Add a hoop on the floor or held at different heights to improve accuracy. Rotate roles.	Stay in groups and areas – practise pass and move skills. On signal how many successful passes can groups make changing position after each pass is made. (No movement with ball allowed – restart count if pass dropped or control is lost). Emphasise the pivot movement.	Groups of 5, 8 x 8 areas, mat and skittle placed in centre, defended by one defender. Rotate roles. Add another skittle, add another defender for 3 *v* 2.	Set up a range of different targets – benches, mats, hops, skittles, circles/targets on walls, etc: free individual practice of aiming and targeting skills. Change ball. Review skills of previous games played in the unit.
Skills Application	'Zig-Zag' Game – 6 Groups: Passing to each member in line – last receiver carries to front and repeated, all move up one place. Development: make into a race of first runner passes to each group member, then next does same, till all have had a go. (Encourage a variety of passes.)	'Bench Ball' Game: set up two groups/two games. Catch and throw/pass and move emphasis (no moving in possession) – all players on a team must play the ball before a score can be made. Team catcher on a mat/bench in a defined area as target (defend one, attack the other).	Develop previous week's game, but this week score through hoop. Emphasise the footwork skills, and the importance of 'pass and move' principles.	2 x Games of 'Skittleball' – Further development of previous week's game, with target now a skittle to knock down placed on a mat (no one allowed on such). Extend exclusion zone – no retained personal possession of ball for more than 3 seconds, no physical contact. Build in notions of attack/defence.	Skittleball games – develop from last week. Add mats, extra skittles to defend, goalkeepers, positional play, rotate positions, etc.	2 x Games of 'Handball' – 2 end D zones, GK only allowed in this area (GK allowed full unrestricted movement here). Using game skills and tactics from previous games score by striking front of bench. Change GKs after a goal is scored.
Cool down	Review skills with class through discussion, and highlight skills to work on in next session.	Individuals with a ball each – find a rebound surface and practise different ways of throwing and catching/retrieving.	Reiterate the footwork skills, further practice as individuals with a ball in their hands.	Back to 8 x 8 areas – skittle placed in middle – aiming skills.	Discuss with class the skills that need working on, technical, tactical, and positional.	Discuss what happened in the games. What could be changed, put into the game to improve its all-round quality? Should we change the targets? The ball? The rules?

Resources	**Assessment:**
Variety of balls (shape, size, texture, density), skittles, hoops, skipping ropes, playground chalk, marker discs/cones, team braid/bibs, etc..	Have passing and receiving skills improved? Is there a greater variety of passes being used? Are footwork skills used in the game situations? Is there a growing appreciation of the tactics required to play the games in a better way? Does the class offer suggestions for improving the games? Where are these skills going to be used in other Invasion Games? Have all the children improved their competence levels within these skills areas? What further practices would help? Are reflexes and reactions improved as a result of this unit of work?

References

General

B.A.A.L.P.E (1995) *Safe Practice in Physical Education.* Dudley: Dudley LEA.

Bray, S. (1993) *Fitness Fun – Promoting Health in P.E.* Crediton: Southgate Publishers.

Bunker, D., Hardy, C., Smith, B. and Almond, L. (1994) *Primary Physical Education – Implementing the National Curriculum.* Cambridge: Cambridge University Press.

Burton, C. and Kent, G. (1993) *Bright Ideas – Inspirations for Physical Education.* Leamington Spa: Scholastic Publications.

Carroll, B. (1994) *Assessment in Physical Education.* Lewes: Falmer Press.

DES (1992) *Physical Education in the National Curriculum.* London: HMSO.

DES (1995) *Physical Education in the National Curriculum.* London: HMSO.

Fisher, R. and Alldridge, D. (1994) *Active PE 1.* Hemel Hempstead: Simon & Schuster Education.

Fisher, R. and Alldridge, D. (1994) *Active PE 2.* Hemel Hempstead: Simon & Schuster Education.

Graham, G. (1992) *Teaching Children Physical Education.* Illinois: Human Kinetics.

Harris, J. and Elbourn, J. (1992) *Warming Up and Cooling Down.* Loughborough: Quorn Litho.

Heath, W., Gregory, C., Money, J., Peat, G., Smith, J. and Stratton, G. (1994) *Physical Education – Key Stage 1.* Cheltenham: Stanley Thornes.

Heath, W., *et al.* (1995) *Physical Education – Key Stage 2.* Cheltenham: Stanley Thornes.

Manners, H.K. and Carroll, M.E. (1995) *A Framework for Physical Education in the Early Years.* Lewes: Falmer Press.

PEAUK, BAALPE, NDTA (1995) *Teaching Physical Education, Key Stages 1 & 2.* Warwick: Warwick Printing Co. Ltd.

Robertson, E. (1994) *Physical Education – A Practical Guide.* London: John Murray Publishers.

Sutcliffe, M. (1993) *Physical Education Activities; Bright Ideas for Early Years.* Leamington Spa: Scholastic Publications.

Wetton, P. (1990) *Physical Education in the Nursery and Infant School.* London: Croom Helm.

Wetton, P. (1987) *Bright Ideas: For Games and P.E.* Leamington Spa: Scholastic Publications.

Wetton, P. (1993) *Practical Guides – Physical Education, Teaching within the National Curriculum.* Leamington Spa: Scholastic Publications.

Health Education

Coonan, W., Worsley, T. and Maynard, T. (1986) *Body Owner's Manual. 1. Health, Lifestyle and Body Systems. 2. Physical Fitness.* South Australia: Life Be In It (Tm)/ Education Department of South Australia.

Health Education Authority (1989) *My Body. A Health Education Authority Project.* Oxford: Heinemann Educational.

Health Education Authority/Thomas Nelson (1989). *Health for Life: The Health Education Authority's Primary School Project.*
1. A Teacher's Planning Guide to Health Education in the Primary School.
2. A Teacher's Guide to Three Key Topics. London: HEA.

Lloyd, J. and Morton, R. (1992) *Health Education Key Stage 1 and Key Stage 2.* (Photocopiable Pupil Resources and Teacher's Resource Books.) Cheltenham: Stanley Thornes.

National Curriculum Council (1990) *Health Education: Curriculum Guidance 5.* York. NCC.

Schools Council (1983) *Fit for Life. Schools Council/HEC Health Education Project for Slow Learners.* London: Macmillan Education.

Sleap, M. and Perch J. (1990) *Happy Heart. 1. Resources for 4–7 Year Olds 2. Resources for 7–11 Year Olds.* London: Health Education Authority/Thomas Nelson.

Williams, T., Wetton, N. and Moon, A. (1989) *A Picture of Health. What do you do that Makes you Healthy and Keeps you Healthy?* London: Health Education Authority.

Williams, T., Wetton, N. and Moon, A. (1989) *A Way In. Five Key Areas of Health Education.* London: Health Education Authority.

Athletics

Cooper, A. (1993) *The Development of Games and Athletic Skills.* Hemel Hempstead: Simon & Schuster.

Couling, D. and Dickinson, D. (1993) *Athletics in the National Curriculum – Key Stage 1.* Birmingham: Amateur Athletic Association of England.

Couling, D. and Dickinson, D. (1993) *Athletics in the National Curriculum – Key Stage 2.* Birmingham: Amateur Athletic Association of England.

Lohmann, W. (1990) *Running, Jumping, Throwing for Youth.* Toronto: Sport Books Publisher.

O'Neil, J. (1996) Athletic Activities for Juniors. London: A & C Black.

Dance

Allen, A. and Coley, J. (1996) *Dance for All 1.* London: David Fulton Publishers.

Allen, A. and Coley, J. (1995) *Dance for All 2.* London: David Fulton Publishers.

Allen, A. and Coley, J. (1995) *Dance for All 3.* London:

David Fulton Publishers.

Bennett, J. P. and Reimer, P. C. (1995) *Rhythmic Activities and Dance.* Leeds: Human Kinetics.

Davies, A. and Sabin, V. (1995) *Body Work; Primary Children, Dance and Gymnastics.* Cheltenham: Stanley Thornes.

Harrison, K. (1993) *Let's Dance – The Place of Dance in the Primary School.* London: Hodder & Stoughton.

Harrison, K., Layton, J. and Morris, M. (1989) *Bright Ideas: Dance and Movement.* Leamington Spa: Scholastic Publications.

Lowden, M. (1989) *Dancing to Learn.* Basingstoke: Falmer Press.

Payne, H. (1990) *Creative Movement and Dance Group Work.* Oxford: Winslow Press.

Purcell, T .M. (1994) *Teaching Children Dance.* Leeds: Human Kinetics.

Rolfe, L. and Harlow, M. (1997) *Let's Look at Dance: Using Professional Dance on Video.* London: David Fulton Publishers.

Shreeves, R. (1985) *Children Dancing.* London: Ward Lock Educational.

Ware, M. (1987) *Time to Dance.* Belair Publications.

Games

Cooper, A. (1988) *The Development of Games Skills.* Oxford: Blackwell.

Cooper, A. (1995) *Starting Games Skills.* Cheltenham: Stanley Thornes.

Don Morris, G. S. and Stiehl, J. (1989) *Changing Kid's Games.* Champaign, Illinois: Human Kinetics Books.

Gustafson, M. and Wolfe, S. (1991) *Great Games For Young People.* Leeds: Human Kinetics.

Hall, J. (1995) *Games for Juniors.* London: A & C Black.

Lenel, P. M. (1984) *Games in the Primary School.* London: Hodder & Stoughton.

Read, B. (1985) *Teaching Children to Play Games – A Resource Pack For Primary Teachers.* Leeds: Coachwise.

Severs, J. (1991) *Activities For P.E Using Small Apparatus.* Oxford: Blackwell.

Severs, J. (1994) *Striking and Fielding Games.* Hemel Hempstead: Simon & Schuster Education.

Sleap, M. (1981) *MiniSport.* London: Heinemann.

Sykes, R. (1990) *Games for Physical Education – A Teacher's Guide.* London: A & C Black.

Gymnastics

Benn, T. and Bern, B. (1992) *Primary Gymnastics A Multi Activities Approach.* Cambridge: Cambridge University Press.

Carroll, M. and Manners, H. (1991) *Gymnastics 7–11, A Session-by-Session Approach to Key Stage 2.* Lewes: Falmer Press.

Hall, J. (1995) *Gymnastic Activities for Juniors.* London: A & C Black.

Jackman, J. and Currier, B. (1992) *Gymnastic Skills & Games.* London: A & C Black.

Long, B. (1982) *Educational Gymnastics, Step by Step.* London: Hodder & Stoughton.

Low, T. (1993) *Gymnastics – Floor, Vault, Beam and Bar.* Marlborough: Crowood Press.

Manners, H. K. and Carroll, M. (1991) *Gymnastics 4–7, Session-By-Session Approach to Key Stage 1.* Lewes: Falmer Press.

Trevor, M. D. (1988) *The Development of Gymnastics Skill.* Oxford: Blackwell.

Williams, J. (1987) *Themes For Educational Gym.* London: A & C Black.

Outdoor and Adventurous Activities

Balazik, D. (1995) *Outdoor & Adventurous Activities for Juniors.* London: A & C Black.

Glover, D. R. and. Midura D. W (1992) *Team Building Through Physical Challenges.* Leeds: Human Kinetics.

Martin, B. (1995) *Hunting the Griz.* Nottingham: Davies Sports.

McNeil, C. (1994) *Orienteering – The Skills of the Game.* Marlborough: Crowood Press.

McNeil, C., Martland, J. and Palmer, P. (1992) *Orienteering in the National Curriculum.* Doune, Perthshire: Harveys.

Renfrew, T. and Michie, D. (eds) (1994) *Orienteering in the 5–14 Scottish Curriculum.* Doune, Perthshire: Harveys.

Swimming

Dyson, M. and Shapland, J. (1992) *The Competent Swimmer.* London: A & C Black.

Eakin, A. (1992) *Swimming – An Illustrated Guide to Teaching Early Practices.* Chorleywood: Published by Anne Eakin.

Journals

British Journal Of Physical Education (published quarterly)

P.E. Primary Focus (published quarterly)

The Bulletin of Physical Education (published 2 to 4 times annually)

LEA Guidelines for PE

A range from across the UK are available from various LEA's – West Sussex, Northern Ireland, Hertfordshire, Coventry, Kent, and Hereford and Worcester are particularly good examples.

Videos

A.E.N.A. Netball For Under 12's.

American Master Teacher Program. *Teaching Children Dance.*

American Master Teacher Program. *Teaching Children Games.*

American Master Teacher Program. *Teaching Children Gymnastics.*
American Master Teacher Program. *Teaching Children Movement Concepts and Skills.*
Australian Sports Commission. *Sport Start.*
B.A.G.A. Rewarding Children's *Fitness for children 3–7.*
B.A.G.A. *Rewarding Children's Fitness for children 7–11*
B.B.C. Education Today Series. *P.E. in the Primary School.*
Brown, A. *Teaching Games to Physically Disabled Children.*
Buckinghamshire County Council. *Educational Gymnastics.*
Coever, W. *Football Coaching.*
Featherstone, G. *Hockey For Juniors.*
L.T.A. *Short Tennis.*
Manchester LEA. *Gymnastics in the Primary School.*
Maude, T. *The Gym Kit.*
R.F.U. *New Image-Mini Rugby.*
Read, B. *Games For 5–6. A Guide For Teachers.*
Sports Council. *Integrated Games.*

Other Resources of practical use

National Governing Bodies of Sport award schemes (Directories available from the Sports Council – Tel. 0171-388-1277).
Know the Game series. London: A & C Black.
Task Cards for Gymnastics, Games and Athletics, Swimming, Dance and Movement, Outdoor Education, and Water Safety (1992) George Austin: Primrose Publishing Ltd.
(Primrose Publishing also produce Policy Guides for PE, Lesson plans, and general guidance materials.)
B.A.G.A. Award schemes materials.
Doncaster Metropolitan Borough Council (1993). *Physical Education – Materials for Implementation of the National Curriculum 5–16.*
Durham LEA and University of Newcastle upon Tyne (1990) *Curriculum Leadership in Physical Education.*
Hereford and Worcester County Council (1991) *The Physical Education Curriculum Leaders' Handbook.*
Persil *'Funfit' National Curriculum Resource Pack for P.E. at KS1 + 2.*
Folens Publishers: *PE Series,* including titles on Gymnastics, Indoor Games, Rugby, Swimming, Netball, Soccer, and Outdoor Games.
Top Play and BT Top Sport packs through Youth Sport Trust (see useful addresses).
Amateur Athletics Association of England can provide information on the 10 Step Award Scheme, 5 Star Athletics, and Cross-Country Running schemes.
Pearson Publishing have produced a set of PE Lesson Plans by Ted Ashford and Carol Dell (1995).

Useful addresses

The Health Education Authority
Hamilton House
Mabledon Place
London WC1X

Department of Education
University of Southampton
Health Education Unit
Southampton S09 5NH
(Director Noreen Wetton)

Curriculum Centre for Physical Education
University of Hull
North Cave
Cottingham
Hull
(Director Mike Sleap)

Department of Physical Education and Sports Science
University of Loughborough
Ashby Road
Loughborough
Leics LE11 3TU
(Director Len Almond)

Youth Sport Trust
Rutland Building
University of Loughborough
Derby Road
Loughborough
Leics LE11 3TV

Schools Health Education Unit
University of Exeter
School of Education
Saint Luke's
Exeter EX1 2LU
(Director John Balding)

Curriculum and Resources Centre
University of Exeter
School of Education
Saint Luke's
Exeter EX1 2LU
(Contact Dr Neil Armstrong)

Physical Education Association of the UK
Suite 5
10 Churchill Square
King's Hill
West Malling
Kent ME19 4OV.

The PEA allows primary schools to join as corporate members, and welcomes primary teachers as individual members.

British Association of Advisers and Lecturers in Physical Education
Nelson House
6 The Beacon Exmouth
Devon EX8 2AG

BAALPE holds, and is responsible for a range of very useful publications and general notes on teaching PE.

National Coaching Foundation
4 College Close
Beckett Park
Leeds lS6 3QM

The Sports Council
16 Upper Woburn Place
London WC1H 0QP

The Sports Council's Information Centre has the addresses and contact numbers of the various sports governing bodies and development officers. A booklet with names and addresses of all major sports governing bodies is available from the information centre on receipt of a stamped addressed envelope. Regional Sports Council offices have more locally relevant information.

National Council for Schools' Sports (NCSS)
Hon Secretary: David Lomas
21, Northampton Road,
Croydon CRO 7HB

The official handbook of the NCSS contains many useful addresses including all the major schools' sports national associations and much useful information. Copies can be obtained from Pat Smith, NCSS Executive Officer, 95 Boxley Drive, West Bridgford, Nottingham, NG2 7GN

British Sports Association For the Disabled
The Mary Glenhaig Suite
Solcast House, 13–27 Brunswick Place
London LN1 6DX

Amateur Swimming Association
Publications Department
Harold Fern House
Derby Square
Loughborough LE11 OAL

Amateur Athletics Association
Edgbaston House
3 Duchess Place, Hagley road
Edgbaston
Birmingham B16 8NM

British Amateur Gymnastics Association
Ford Hall
Lilleshall National Sports Centre
Newport
Shropshire TF10 9NB.

The Football Association
16 Lancaster Gate
London W2 3LW

The Rugby Football Union
Twickenham
Middlesex
TW1 1EW.

The All England Netball Association
Netball House
9 Paynes Park
Hitchin
Herts SG5 1EH

The Hockey Association
Norfolk House
102 Saxon Gate West
Milton Keynes MK9 2EP

The National Cricket Association
Lords Cricket Ground
London NW8 8QN

National Association For Outdoor Education
Barbara Humberstone (Secretary)
251 Woodlands Road
Southampton
SO4 2GS

The British Orienteering Federation
Riversdale
Dale Road North
Darley Dale
Matlock
Derbyshire DE4 2HX

St John's Ambulance
Suppies Department
Priory House
St John's Gate
Clerkenwell
London EC1M 4PA

Appendix

Core Equipment for PE Activities

Throwing and catching/sending and receiving equipment

Beanbags
Balloons
Quoits
Table tennis balls
Shuttlecocks
Airflow balls
Sponge balls – assorted sizes, shapes, textures, bounce potential
Rubber balls
Rounders balls – plastic, leather
Cricket balls – lightweight, indoor, pudding,composition, leather
Stoolballs
Softballs
Sequence/Utility balls with symbols, numbers, letters marked
Footballs – size 3 and 4
Rugby balls – size 3 and 4
Dice shapes – dot marked
Basketballs – micro and mini
Tennis balls – low bounce, regular
Netballs – size 3 and 4
Hockey balls – indoor and outdoor
Plastic balls – sizes 2, 3 and 4
Pucks – plastic
Foam javelins, shot and discus

Striking and fielding equipment

Padder bats – wooden and plastic, different shapes, long and short handled
Cricket bats – junior sizes
Tennis rackets – short tennis style, plastic
Badminton rackets
Rounders bats
Shinty sticks
Unihoc sticks
Hockey sticks – range of sizes
Stoolball bats
Softball bats

Gymnastic equipment

Fixed apparatus – window frames, 'cave' type, with additional ladders, bars, poles and hoop attachments
Set of rope pulleys – also rope ladders, rings, hoops
Mats – various shapes, size, weight and thickness conducive to the age range
Benches – short and long, padded too, with hook attachments preferably at both ends
Wooden planks – hook attachments at both ends
Agility table – round/hexagonal, padded top
Nesting tables – ideally 5, from 80 cm progressing higher
Bar box – 2 sections
Section box – 3 part
Wooden stools – various heights
Balance beams – low to floor
Beat boards – ideally 2 different types
Foam equipment – various shapes and sizes
(Other everyday PE equipment can also be used for essential basic skills, like skittles and cones, skipping ropes, jumping canes, etc)

Miscellaneous

Badminton nets
Utility stands and posts
Marker cones and discs
Wooden skittles – small and large
Wire skittles
Cricket stumps – individual and spring-set
Rounders posts
Stoolball posts
Wooden canes – for jumping and hurdling practises
Hoops – wooden and plastic
Team braid – primary colours
Team bibs – primary colours
Kwik Cricket set
Batinton set
Short Tennis set
Unihoc set
Mini Athletics set
Marker flags and pegs
Skipping ropes – various lengths
Playground chalk
Ball pump(s) and adaptors
Relay batons
Stopwatches
Measuring tapes
Jumping stands, weighted rope, flexi-bar, round section cross-bar
Netball posts (adjustable heights)
'Five-a-side' soccer goals
Mini basketball posts and nets (adjustable heights)
Ribbons
Compasses
Clipboards
Containers – trolleys, stands, nets, bags, boxes, crates, etc.

Dance/movement

Access to a good quality cassette player/sound system, appropriate tapes, and a range of good percussion instruments are all invaluable teaching aids. Poetry books will lend additional ideas and stimulation to lessons. Themes and topics central to class planning will provide lots of movement ideas too. The use of ribbons and balloons, feathers and scarves to illustrate movement potential in familiar guise will further support such sessions.